GAY
Rights

**TRICIA
ANDRYSZEWSKI**

Twenty-First Century Books
Brookfield, Connecticut

Photographs courtesy of © Bettye Lane: pp. 8, 14, 25; UPI/Corbis-Bettmann: pp. 15, 19 (top), 40, 63 (top); AP/Wide World Photos: pp. 17, 19 (bottom), 44, 63 (bottom), 71, 73, 84; Impact Visuals: pp. 20 (© Rick Reinhard), 54 (© Rick Gerharter), 58 (© Rick Gerharter); Liaison Agency: pp. 37 (© Karl Gehring), 68 (© 1996 Don Tracy), 93 (© Evan Agostini); Corbis/Reuters: p. 45; Corbis/Bettmann: p. 50; © Jay Mallin: p. 76

Library of Congress Cataloging-in-Publication Data
Andryszewski, Tricia, 1956–
Gay rights / Tricia Andryszewski
p. cm.
Includes bibliographical references and index.
Summary: Traces the history of the gay rights movement in America, from the Stonewall riots to the legal and societal status of gay rights at the turn of the century.
ISBN 0-7613-1568-3 (lib. bdg.)
1. Gay rights—United States—History—Juvenile literture.
2. Gay liberation movement—United States—History—Juvenile literature. [1. Gay rights—History. 2. Gay liberation movement—History. 3. homosexuality.] I. Title.
HQ76.8.U5 A664 2000
305.9'0664—dc21   99-048185

Published by Twenty-First Century Books,
A Division of The Millbrook Press
2 Old New Milford Road, Brookfield, CT   06804
www.millbrookpress.com

Contents

GAY
Rights

A plaque at the site of the Stonewall Inn was
dedicated seven years after the unexpected riot
that sparked the gay rights movement.

The Stonewall Riots

"Christopher Street belongs to the queens."

—chanted by crowd at the Stonewall riots[1]

At 3:00 A.M. on June 28, 1969, New York City police raided the Stonewall Inn, a bar catering to homosexuals, on Christopher Street in the city's bohemian Greenwich Village section. The raid itself, for alleged violation of liquor laws, was not unusual. Police often targeted such bars and their patrons for harassment. But what followed was very unusual. Instead of passively allowing the police to shut the bar down, as the police expected and as homosexuals had typically done in the past, the bar's patrons and sympathizers from the neighborhood fought back. They threw trash at the police and rioted for nearly an hour.

For several nights running, crowds gathered in the Village to protest the Stonewall raid, clashing with police. Over the next few weeks the riots were followed by larger, more peaceful protest rallies.

The Stonewall riots were a turning point in how homosexuality has been perceived and treated in the United States. Before Stonewall, homosexual sex (even in one's own home) was illegal in every state except Illinois. Known homosexuals were banned from many professions, from teaching to law, medicine, the armed forces—even hairdressing in many states. And nowhere in the country did any law or public policy protect homosexuals from discrimination in jobs, housing, or such public accommodations as restaurants and hotels.[2]

Stonewall both marked and inspired a growing new openness about sexual orientation. In the months and years to come, unprecedented numbers of gay men and lesbians would openly identify themselves, organize themselves, and demand civil rights and greater public acceptance of homosexuality.

The Gay Rights Movement in America: An Overview

"I can't conceive the hidden life anymore, don't think of it as life. When you finally come out, there's a pain that stops, and you know it will never hurt like that again."
—gay memoirist Paul Monette[1]

The gay rights movement didn't just suddenly appear out of nowhere after the Stonewall raid and riots. Homosexuality has been a fact of life through all of human history, sometimes tolerated, occasionally celebrated, often condemned. In the mid-1960s, inspired by the successes of the black civil rights movement, groups of gay men and lesbians had begun to fight antihomosexual discrimination. At the same time, as part of the general climate of tolerance and permissiveness that swept the country in the 1960s and early 1970s, various mainstream American organizations announced their opposition to laws against homosexual sex and other forms of discrimination against homosexuals. These organizations included the American Civil Liberties

Union in 1967, the American Sociological Association in 1969, the Lutheran Church in 1970, the American Bar Association in 1973, and many more.

The new burst of gay rights activism ushered in by Stonewall was closely related to other protest and youth "liberation" movements of the time: antiwar, black power, women's liberation. Like the other liberation movements, gay liberation was often flamboyant, in-your-face, and outrageous. This phase of the gay rights movement focused less on civil rights and more on personal liberation. The idea was to free your mind to believe that "gay is good" and accept your own homosexuality, to "come out" and acknowledge it openly, and to transform the world by transforming individual lives.

This "Homosexual Bill of Rights" was adopted by the North American Conference of Homophile Organizations in August 1968:

BASIC RIGHTS

1. Private consensual sex between persons over the age of consent shall not be an offense.
2. Solicitation for any sexual acts shall not be an offense except upon the filing of a complaint by the aggrieved party, not a police officer or agent.
3. A person's sexual orientation or practice shall not be a factor in the granting or renewing of federal security clearances or visas, or in the granting of citizenship.
4. Service in and discharge from the Armed Forces and eligibility for veteran's benefits shall be without reference to homosexuality.
5. A person's sexual orientation or practice shall not affect his eligibility for employment with federal, state, or local governments, or private employers.

AREAS FOR IMMEDIATE REFORM

1. Police and other government agents shall cease the practice of enticement and entrapment of homosexuals.
2. Police shall desist from notifying the employers of those arrested for homosexual offenses.
3. Neither the police department nor any other government agency shall keep files solely for the purpose of identifying homosexuals.
4. The practice of harassing bars and other establishments and of revoking their licenses because they cater to homosexuals shall cease.
5. The practice of reviewing less-than-honorable military discharges, granted for homosexual orientation or practice, shall be established, with the goal of upgrading them into fully honorable discharges.
6. The registration of sex offenders shall not be required.
7. City ordinances involving sexual matters shall be rescinded and these matters left to state legislatures.
8. Conviction for homosexual offenses shall not be the basis for prohibiting issuance of professional or any other licenses nor for the revocation of these licenses.
9. No questions regarding sexual orientation or practice shall appear on application forms, personnel data sheets, or in personal interviews.
10. No government agency shall use the classification of homosexuality as an alleged illness to limit the freedom, rights, or privileges of any homosexual.[2]

Gay liberation dominated the gay rights movement from 1969 through the early 1970s. In 1970 a "gay pride" parade in New York City drew about 10,000 marchers.[3]

An early gay pride parade in New York City—in the first few years of the movement, gay liberation was the focus.

By the end of the following year, gay liberation groups had sprung up in just about every large city and college campus across the United States.[4]

A notable success of the gay liberationists was their challenge to the American medical establishment's view of homosexuality. For much of this century, doctors considered homosexuality a kind of disease. In 1974, after a sustained campaign of protest and pressure, the American Psychiatric Association removed homosexuality from its list of medical diseases and disorders. The consensus among American medical authorities today is that homosexual orientation (sexual attraction to members of the same sex) is an unchangeable characteristic—not a medical disorder—established either before birth or in very early childhood.

The gay liberation movement had widespread effects even for gay men and lesbians who never joined a protest march or consciousness-raising group. With more homosexuals out and in the public eye, gay pride and self-acceptance became easier to imagine and own. Highly visible gay communities gathered in cities around the

Marchers in the 1974 parade that ended Gay Pride Week in New York City

nation: not only in San Francisco and New York but also in Chicago, Houston, Miami, Philadelphia, Seattle, and other places. Greater gay visibility fueled the growth of a new gay, chiefly male marketplace of bars and discos, vacation destinations, even doctors and lawyers and other service providers catering to a gay clientele.

The cultural ferment that gave rise to gay and other liberation groups subsided in the mid-1970s. But the push for gay rights didn't fade away. Instead, the increasingly visible and organized gay community shifted toward seeking political and legal reic. ns and full acceptance in the workplace, housing, and such mainstream institutions as churches.

Beginning in 1974, liberal representatives repeatedly proposed (and Congress rejected) amending the national Civil Rights Act to extend federal government protection against discrimination to homosexuals. Blocked at the national level, gay rights activists had more success at the state and local level: By the late 1970s several dozen local communities had adopted some form of gay antidiscrimination protection.[5] Most of these communities were university towns, plus a few large cities (Detroit, Minneapolis, San Francisco, Seattle, and Washington) with organized gay and lesbian communities.[6]

Much of the American public seemed ready to accept at least some such changes. As early as 1977, more than half believed that homosexuals should have equal rights in job opportunities, while only a third believed that they shouldn't.[7]

Backlash However, in the late 1970s, a widely publicized backlash emerged against homosexuality in general and gay rights in particular. A small minority passionately opposed to homosexuality began to compete with gay rights activists for the hearts

Anita Bryant headed up a successful crusade to nullify a gay rights ordinance in Florida in 1977.

and votes of the vast numbers of Americans who had never given much thought to the matter. This competitive struggle has continued ever since.

The best-known early opponent of gay rights was Anita Bryant. A Christian evangelical singer, Bryant was known nationally for her appearances in commercials for Florida orange juice. When Dade County, Florida (which includes Miami), passed an ordinance prohibiting discrimination against homosexuals, Bryant and her organization mounted a campaign to repeal the ordinance. Matching the harsh tone of much subsequent gay rights debate, Bryant referred to homosexuality as a "perverse and dangerous" way of life. The campaign brought together a coalition of national as well as local conservative politicians and religious leaders, and it drew nation-wide financial support and publicity from conservative Christian TV programming. In June 1977 the Dade County gay rights ordinance was repealed.

The new antigay coalition followed up its victory in Dade County with several successful repeals in other cities of similar civil rights measures covering sexual orientation. But the Dade County repeal rallied gay rights activists, too.

The most widely publicized debate about gay rights in the aftermath of the Dade County repeal took place in California, especially in San Francisco, where a large and highly visible gay population had settled. In 1978 the entire state of California debated an antigay ballot initiative sponsored by the conservative State Senator John Briggs. Proposition 6 (also known as the Briggs Initiative) called for the firing of all homosexual teachers and any teacher speaking favorably about homosexuality in a public school classroom. Harvey Milk, a newly elected, openly gay San Francisco city supervisor, debated Briggs and other antigay advocates around the state. After a hard-fought campaign fueled by contributions from religious conservatives and gay rights supporters all over the United States, California voters defeated Proposition 6 in November 1978.

Weeks later Harvey Milk and gay-friendly Mayor George Moscone were shot to death in their offices at San Francisco's City Hall by an antigay former city supervisor, Dan White. Gay (and other) San Franciscans voiced their shock and sorrow at a candlelit memorial march to City Hall. Five months later sorrow turned to outrage when Dan White, convicted of manslaughter by a jury with no gay members, was sentenced to less than eight years in prison for the two killings. That night rioters at City Hall smashed windows and set fire to police cars; more than 120 people were injured, and property damage exceeded $1 million.

This photo of Harvey Milk (left) and San Francisco Mayor George Moscone was taken in April 1978 as the mayor signed a gay rights ordinance. Both men were shot and killed seven months later.

A spontaneous outpouring of grief over slain Mayor George Moscone and supervisor Harvey Milk turned into a candlelight vigil.

Congressman Barney Frank acknowledged in 1987 that he was gay.

Far from scaring homosexuals back into "the closet" (a life of hiding homosexuality and pretending publicly to be heterosexual), the Milk/Moscone murders and the antigay political campaigns made activists of many gay men and lesbians who had previously kept to the sidelines. In 1979 at least 100,000 demonstrators attended the First National Gay and Lesbian Civil Rights March on Washington, D.C.[8] Over the next several years, homosexuals became ever more visible in public life and gay rights became a more prominent issue nationally as well as in many localities:

- Between 1979 and 1981, California Governor Jerry Brown appointed four openly homosexual state judges.[9]

- In 1980 a gay teenage boy in Providence, Rhode Island, successfully sued his high school for the right to bring a male date to his senior prom.[10]
- The 1980 Democratic party platform supported passage of federal gay rights legislation.[11]
- In 1983 a federal judge found the Immigration and Naturalization Service's policy of excluding homosexuals from the country to be unconstitutional. (Congress finally voted to end the policy in 1990.)[12]

Gay rights laws offer a striking indication of how widely the debate about gay rights reached in these years: By the mid-1980s, more than fifty U.S. cities and several states had included sexual orientation in local or state human rights measures. This was no steady march of progress, though. While these measures were being enacted, dozens of other communities either refused or repealed similar measures.[13]

Opponents of gay rights measures drew support from a broad-based conservative backlash against what many Americans considered the excesses and immorality displayed by popular youth culture since the 1960s. Beginning in the 1970s and gaining widespread public support in the more conservative 1980s, antiabortion, antiwomen's lib, antipornography, and antigay campaigns overlapped and found supporters among the same pool of conservative Americans.

Prominent among these conservatives were evangelical Christians—nearly a quarter of the U.S. population. The various "anti" campaigns drew increasing numbers of evangelicals into political activism, often through such religious/political organizations as the Reverend Jerry Falwell's Moral Majority (founded in 1979) and, later, the Christian Coalition. This block of "religious right" voters and activists became more and more important in

Roger Magnuson, a writer influential among religious right Christians is by no means the most harshly condemning critic of gay rights. However, in the following excerpts from one of his books he does typify the personal and emotional tone of religious right rhetoric and touches upon some of the most common points made by the religious right concerning homosexuality:

"Militant homosexuals are on the march. Their goal is total social acceptance and legal sanction of their behavior and lifestyle, and they have made inroads seemingly everywhere....

"Most people opposed to gay rights first react with an instinctive revulsion. Homosexuals call this distaste 'homophobia,' but it is only the natural revulsion a normal person feels in the face of sexual perversion....

"Put simply, to those who believe that the Bible is the Word of God, homosexuality is immoral because God says so. But even were there no explicit command in the Bible that forbade sodomy, it is easy to show that it is an unnatural act— whether by examining basic anatomy, hygiene, the physical and psychological consequences for homosexuals themselves, the promiscuity and exploitation built into 'normal' homosexual behavior, or by merely a head count of the world's religions....

"Because homosexuality is an offense against nature as well as against revealed religion, it is properly legislated against by lawmakers....

"The sodomite is trapped in a lust that is destroying him by inches and yards. To tell him he cannot help himself, to tell him to rejoice in his fatal disease, is to consign him forever to unhappiness....

"Gay rights laws that give special protections and privileges to people who practice sexual perversion are little more than a reward for immorality....

"As a group, homosexuals release both disease and crime into society to an extent far in excess of their percentage of the population....

"The existence of public homosexuality in our times has a powerful influence on the kind of society we have—the clothes we wear, the music we listen to, the preaching we hear from our pulpits, the treatment given our children, the lives lived by homosexuals themselves...the latent homosexuals recruited into overt conduct....

"Homosexuals have a vision of the future far outside the mainstream of American life...where all sexual activity is placed beyond the rule of moral norms. The final destination for this ideology is a city of polymorphous and perverse sexuality where anything goes....

"What is at stake is not some modest inclusion in an obscure municipal human rights ordinance but children, the family, and civilization itself."[14]

American politics as it came to dominate the Republican party in the 1980s and 1990s. (As early as the 1984 election campaign, President Ronald Reagan voiced Republican solidarity with the religious right by vowing to "resist the efforts of some to obtain government endorsement of homosexuality.")[15] The religious right also has been the dominant voice against gay rights.

AIDS Crisis Although the AIDS virus first infiltrated America's gay community sometime in the 1970s, the earliest reports of a mysterious, deadly sickness afflicting gay men in the United States emerged in 1981. News of the disease spread through the gay community in 1982 and among the general public in the mid-1980s. AIDS, especially in the early years of the epidemic when its cause and mode of transmission were still unclear, set off a wave of homophobia and antigay discrimination. Some medical personnel refused to treat AIDS patients. Some ambulance workers and police refused to touch patients who appeared to be gay. Some funeral homes refused to handle AIDS cases.

The revelation, in 1985, that movie star Rock Hudson was gay and ill with AIDS marked a turning point in public attitudes. Far from turning against Hudson, public opinion was overwhelmingly compassionate—and his homosexuality irrelevant to that compassion. Furthermore, the cause of the disease and the ways it could and could not be transmitted were by then more clearly understood. It had become known that this wasn't a "gay disease"—heterosexuals were infecting one another, too. Americans came to see AIDS as a disease like any other, requiring funding for research, treatment, and prevention—and compassion for its victims.

Because of the AIDS epidemic and the gay community's response to it, gay men became the focus of more, often positive, media attention than ever before. And in many ways Americans demonstrated growing acceptance of homosexuals in public life and in the workplace:

- In 1987, Congressman Barney Frank (D-Mass.) acknowledged that he was gay. His constituents have returned him to Congress in several elections since then.
- In 1991 a black lesbian, Sherry Harris, was elected mayor of Seattle.
- By the early 1990s, U.S. companies as diverse as the Lotus software company, Levi Strauss, the

Many feel the government has no business making laws about the most intimate details of a person's life.

Boston Globe, and the Apple computer company had granted spousal benefits to same-sex partners of their homosexual employees.[16]

- Also by the early 1990s, most of the largest U.S. companies had adopted formal nondiscrimination policies covering gay men and lesbians. (Most smaller companies, however, had no such formal policies.)[17]

The AIDS epidemic drew unprecedented numbers of gay men out of the closet and increased the visibility of the gay community. (By 1993 a majority of Americans polled said they knew at least one homosexual personally, up from just 25 to 30 percent in 1985.)[18] AIDS also diverted a lot of the gay community's energy into the struggle to raise money for AIDS research and to prevent more infections—and into the exhausting work of taking care of the sick and dying. It also made sex with many partners less attractive and committed monogamous relationships more attractive and admired among gay men—a change that would soon fuel a growing demand for legal domestic partnership and marriage rights. In the 1990s, with fewer gay men becoming infected and the life spans for many Americans with AIDS lengthening, the gay rights movement increasingly returned its attention to civil rights and public acceptance issues.

Gay Rights Laws

"What are you doing in my bedroom?"

—Michael Hardwick to policeman
about to arrest him for having sex
with another man in his own home.[1]

Gay rights activists have joined together with civil libertarians to challenge state sodomy laws, which make homosexual sex illegal. They also have sought for homosexuals the same kinds of civil rights protections extended to racial and other protected minorities. In addition, gay rights activists have fought against efforts by antigay activists to enact state and local antigay legislation.

Sodomy Laws

State sodomy laws (there is no such law at the federal level) make it a crime for consenting adults to engage in oral or anal sex. Some laws have been written so that they apply to homosexuals only; others apply equally to heterosexuals.

Gay rights activists haven't been alone in seeking an end to sodomy laws. Civil liberties activists, most notably the American Civil Liberties Union (ACLU), have opposed sodomy laws as an unwarranted restriction on personal liberty and a state invasion of privacy. In recent years advocates for the disabled also have denounced sodomy laws on the grounds that they make illegal the only kinds of sex feasible for many wheelchair-bound individuals. In addition, some legal experts have spoken out against sodomy laws on the grounds that any law that most people break gives police and prosecutors a dangerous, arbitrary power.

Sodomy laws are rarely enforced, but when they are enforced they are nearly always used against gay men or lesbians, most often against gay men caught having sex in public or semipublic places. Occasionally they have been used against gay men or lesbians having sex in their own bedrooms. Since homosexual partners can be presumed to be violating such a law, sodomy laws put gay men and lesbians at continual risk for arbitrary arrest. They also have been used to justify discrimination against homosexuals in custody and employment disputes.

Rarely, sodomy laws have been used to prosecute heterosexuals, typically in difficult sexual assault cases. When an alleged rapist claims his victim consented to sex and describes an act of sodomy, prosecutors unsure of their ability to win conviction on the assault charge have in some cases asked juries for a sodomy conviction instead.

These rare cases are the chief legal reason cited to justify keeping sodomy laws in effect. Most advocates of sodomy laws, however, have been motivated chiefly by moral beliefs rather than legal factors: They believe that homosexual behavior is wrong and that the state should discourage it.

In 1968 every state except Illinois had sodomy laws in effect. In the 1970s many states repealed their sodomy laws as part of broader legal housecleaning efforts intended to eliminate obsolete legal codes. Other state sodomy laws have been struck down in court.

One court challenge worked its way up to the U.S. Supreme Court. In August 1982, Michael Hardwick was charged with breaking a Georgia sodomy law by having sex with another man in the bedroom of his own home. (The law specified that a "person commits the offense of sodomy when he performs or submits to any sexual act involving the sex organs of one person and the mouth or anus of another.")[2] Although the district attorney decided not to prosecute Hardwick, Hardwick sued the state, claiming that the state's sodomy law was unconstitutional.

In 1986 the Supreme Court decided against Hardwick. "The issue presented [by Hardwick]," Justice Byron White wrote for the court, in *Bowers* v. *Hardwick*, "is whether the Federal Constitution confers a fundamental right upon homosexuals to engage in sodomy and hence invalidates the laws of the many States that still make such conduct illegal and have done so for a very long time.... [Hardwick] would have us announce...a fundamental right to engage in homosexual sodomy. This we are quite unwilling to do."[3]

Four of the Supreme Court's nine justices sharply disagreed with Justice White's majority opinion. Writing for the four dissenters, Justice Harry Blackmun asserted that "this case is about 'the most comprehensive of rights and the right most valued by civilized men,' namely, 'the right to be let alone.'...The Court claims that its decision today merely refuses to recognize a fundamental right to engage in homosexual sodomy; what the Court really has refused to recognize is the fundamental interest all individuals have in controlling the nature of their intimate associations with others.... Indeed, the right of an individual to conduct intimate relationships in the intimacy of his or her own home seems to me to be the heart of the Constitution's protection of privacy."[4]

Although the Supreme Court refused to categorically strike down all sodomy laws, it left the states free to act on their own, and many have done so—including Georgia. In November 1998, Georgia's highest court struck down the same sodomy law upheld in *Bowers* on the grounds that it violated the *state's* constitution. By then, a total of seven state courts had similarly struck down sodomy laws, and twenty-five state legislatures had repealed them. Court challenges were under way in several other states.[5]

As of December 1999, only eighteen states had laws against sodomy in force. Five prohibited same-sex sodomy only (Texas, Oklahoma, Kansas, Arkansas, and Missouri). Thirteen prohibited both heterosexual and homosexual sodomy (Arizona, Utah, Idaho, Minnesota, Michigan, Louisiana, Mississippi, Alabama, Florida, South Carolina, North Carolina, Virginia, and Massachusetts).[6]

Gay Rights Laws

"Gay rights" laws typically involve adding "sexual orientation" to a list of categories against which discrimination is prohibited by civil rights law. Such a measure might, for example, ban discrimination on the basis of race, religion, national origin, handicapped status, or sexual preference by a local government hiring its employees or providing services. Some measures prohibit private citizens as well as the government from discriminating in such activities as renting an apartment, hiring an employee, serving customers in a restaurant, or providing other forms of "public accommodation."

Gay rights antidiscrimination measures most commonly ban discrimination in employment by local or state government. A majority of such measures have also banned discrimination in private rental housing (often with an exemption for buildings with only a few units), in public accommodations, in private employment, and by private contractors working for the government. Some measures ban discrimination by credit agencies. Very few measures ban other forms of discrimination (by schools or unions, for example).[7]

Gay rights advocates say that laws banning discrimination against homosexuals are needed for the same reasons as laws banning discrimination against other minorities—that gay men and lesbians need the law to protect them from being denied equal treatment because of their sexual orientation. Without such laws, homosexuals denied jobs or housing because they're gay can't go to court to demand equal treatment. Opponents of gay rights laws contend that homosexuals already enjoy the full range of rights granted to all other citizens, that special gay rights laws aren't needed, and that such laws unjustly create special privileges for homosexuals.

Antigay rights advocates have often raised the issue of affirmative action, suggesting that gay rights laws could require a local government or even private employers to hire enough homosexuals to meet a quota. Such requirements typically are not written into civil rights antidiscrimination measures but sometimes have been ordered by a court or triggered by other legislation intended to address persistent patterns of discrimination against protected racial minorities. Some gay rights measures have specifically disallowed affirmative action on the basis of sexual orientation, and no gay rights measure has yet led to any affirmative action program. In addition, gay rights and other antidiscrimination measures often explicitly exempt religious organizations, so that a church school, for example, cannot be required to hire a homosexual teacher—nor can a church be required to ordain homosexual ministers.

Controversy has also arisen concerning what constitutes a "public accommodation" covered by antidiscrimination law. For example, the Boy Scouts of America have been sued in several states for illegal discrimination because they exclude homosexuals, agnostics, and atheists. The Boy Scouts contend they are a private club not subject to state or local antidiscrimination laws; their challengers contend they are in fact a public accommodation. In March 1998 a New Jersey court found that the Boy Scouts were a public accommodation—and a California court ruled that they were not. Other cases against the Boy Scouts were pending elsewhere. In January 2000, the U.S. Supreme Court agreed to decide the New Jersey case.[8]

National civil rights legislation does not cover sexual orientation. Amendment of the federal Civil Rights Act to prohibit antigay discrimination has been repeatedly proposed (since 1974) but not passed by Congress.

At the state level, as of December 1999, eleven states had in effect some form of civil rights laws covering sexual orientation: Wisconsin (enacted in 1982); Massachusetts (1989); Hawaii and Connecticut (1991); New Jersey, California, and Vermont (1992); Minnesota (1993); Rhode Island (1995); New Hampshire (1997); and Nevada (1999). Maine passed a statewide gay rights law in 1997 then repealed it in 1998. Also in 1998 the state of Oregon's appeals court extended that state's ban on workplace discrimination to cover sexual orientation. And in October 1999, California strengthened its gay rights laws with three measures concerning domestic partners (gay or straight), discrimination in employment and housing, and discrimination in public schools.[9]

Locally, as of December 1998, measures banning antigay discrimination were in force in 27 counties and 136 cities.[10] Although all kinds of communities have adopted gay rights measures, most typically these have

GAY RIGHTS LAWS

In 1972, East Lansing, Michigan, became the first U.S. city to adopt a nondiscrimination policy covering sexual orientation. Here are some excerpts: "It is hereby declared to be contrary to the public policy of the City of East Lansing for any person to deny any other person the enjoyment of his/her civil rights or for any person to discriminate against any other person in the exercise of his/her civil rights or to harass any person because of religion, race, color, national origin, age, height, weight, handicap, sex, marital status, sexual orientation, student status, or because of the use by an individual of adaptive devices or aids....

"Employment...It is unlawful for an employer to...limit, segregate, classify, fail or refuse to hire, to recruit, to discharge, or otherwise discriminate against an individual with respect to employment...because of...sexual orientation....

"Housing...The opportunity to...engage in any...type of real estate transaction...is hereby recognized and declared to be a civil right. This includes but is not limited to seeking, inspecting, advertising, offering or listing of real property without discrimination because of...sexual orientation....

"Public accommodation...A person shall not deny an individual the full and equal enjoyment of...a place of public accommodation or public service because of...sexual orientation."[11]

In 1981, Wisconsin became the first state to adopt a statewide nondiscrimination law covering sexual orientation. Excerpts follow: "All persons shall have an equal opportunity for housing regardless of sex, race, color, sexual orientation, handicap, religion, national origin, sex or marital status..., lawful source of income, age or ancestry and it is the duty of the local units of government to assist in the orderly prevention or removal of all discrimination in housing....

"It is declared to be the public policy of the state to encourage and foster to the fullest extent practicable the employment of all properly qualified persons regardless of...sexual orientation. Nothing in this subsection requires an affirmative action program."

A person is guilty of a Class A Misdemeanor who "denies to another or charges another a higher price than the regular rate for the full and equal enjoyment of any public place of accommodation or amusement because of...sexual orientation...[or] gives preferential treatment to some classes of persons in providing services or facilities...because of...sexual orientation."[12]

been larger cities in the Northeast and on the West Coast with large liberal Protestant populations and where local gay/lesbian community organizations are active, especially in coalition with civil rights groups, women's groups, liberal churches, etc.[13]

In 1972, East Lansing, Michigan, was the first municipality to adopt a gay rights antidiscrimination measure. Some municipalities have passed such measures and later repealed them. Dade County, which passed a gay rights law then repealed it following Anita Bryant's much-publicized antigay campaign in 1977, passed gay rights legislation again in 1998.

All of the repeal efforts and many of the efforts to pass gay rights legislation have generated heated debate between gay rights and antigay advocates. Both sides have typically drawn on national support and funding networks as well as grass roots support.

Antigay Rights Laws

Antigay rights activists not only have fought to defeat and repeal gay rights measures. They also have proposed various measures explicitly permitting or mandating discrimination against homosexuals or forbidding state and local governments from including sexual orientation in the categories covered by antidiscrimination legislation.

The defeated 1978 Briggs Initiative in California (see Chapter 1) was followed by a variety of other state and local antigay rights proposals in the late 1970s and 1980s. The pace of these initiatives picked up in the early 1990s. In 1992, Cincinnati voters passed one nationally noted antigay rights measure, and Colorado voters approved another (known as Amendment 2).[14] Idaho and Maine voters defeated statewide antigay rights measures in 1994 and 1995.

Oregon voters passed an antigay measure in 1988 that was challenged and ultimately defeated in court. Yet the antigay activists persisted. In 1992, Oregon considered and debated Proposition 9, a measure forbidding state government from protecting, promoting, or expressing approval of homosexuality. According to Lon Mabon, founder of Oregon Citizens Alliance, which spearheaded the effort to pass Proposition 9: "Most of society is willing to tolerate a subculture built around a homosexual life style. What we want to do is establish a barrier. The state must ultimately say that homosexuality is wrong.... Cultural diversity is the buzzword being used to make homosexuals full-fledged minorities that require civil rights protection. Homosexuality is not a civil right, but an aberration."[15]

After Oregon voters defeated Proposition 9 in 1992, antigay activists set to work on local ordinances based on the failed statewide measure. More than a dozen Oregon towns and counties eventually enacted such measures.[16] In May 1992, Springfield, Oregon, adopted a city law prohibiting the local government from taking actions to establish gay rights. Here's an excerpt: "The City of Springfield…shall not make, pass, adopt, or enforce any law, ordinance, rule, or resolution that recognizes any categorical provisions such as 'sexual orientation,' 'sexual preference,' and similar phrases that includes [sic] homosexuality, pedophilia, sadism, or masochism, nor shall the City of Springfield, its agencies, departments, bureaus, properties, or monies be used to promote, encourage, or facilitate homosexuality, pedophilia, sadism, or masochism."[17] (Statewide, however, Oregon voters again rejected an antigay initiative in 1994.)

Similar measures have been proposed in states and localities across the country. Even those that have been voted down or struck down by courts have cost gay rights activists a lot of time and money in fighting them— resources they'd rather expend working to repeal sodomy laws or pass antidiscrimination legislation.

The U.S. Supreme Court's position on antigay laws has been confusing. Early on, in 1985, the Supreme Court struck down an Oklahoma law similar to the Briggs Initiative mandating the firing of gay and lesbian teachers and prohibiting favorable mention of homosexuality in public schools.[18]

Colorado voters in 1992 passed Amendment 2, an antigay rights amendment to the state's constitution: "Neither the State of Colorado, through any of its branches or departments, nor any of its agencies, political subdivisions, municipalities or school districts, shall enact, adopt or enforce any statute, regulation, ordinance or policy whereby homosexual, lesbian or bisexual orientation, conduct, practices or relationships shall constitute or otherwise be the basis of, or entitle any person or class of persons to have or claim any minority status, quota preferences, protected status or claim of discrimination."[19]

Gay rights advocates celebrated the Supreme
Court's ruling that Colorado's antigay
Amendment 2 was unconstitutional.

In 1996, in *Romer* v. *Evans*, the court affirmed a lower court ruling that struck down Colorado's Amendment 2, asserting that the U.S. Constitution does not permit a state to strip a whole class of citizens (homosexuals) of legal protections. Justice Anthony Kennedy wrote for the court:

> "We cannot accept the view that Amendment 2...does no more than deprive homosexuals of special rights. To the contrary, the amendment imposes a special disability upon those persons alone....
>
> It is not within our constitutional tradition to enact laws of this sort. Central both to the idea of the rule of law and to our own Constitution's guarantee of equal protection is the principle that government and each of its parts remain open on impartial terms to all who seek its assistance....
>
> Amendment 2 classifies homosexuals not to further a proper legislative end but to make them unequal to everyone else. This Colorado cannot do. A State cannot so deem a class of persons a stranger to its laws."[20]

Two years later, however, in 1998, the Supreme Court let stand (by refusing to hear the case) Cincinnati's measure banning local gay rights legislation. Lower courts had found the Cincinnati measure vaguely worded and limited to "special protection" and thus less sweeping than Amendment 2. Several Supreme Court justices emphasized that their refusal to hear the Cincinnati case should not be read as a statement on underlying gay rights issues.[21] It appears likely that the court will revisit antigay rights law in the future.

Gays in the Military

"When I was in the military, they gave me a medal for killing two men, and a discharge for loving one."
—Sgt. Leonard Matlovich,
awarded the Bronze Star, Purple Heart, and other
commendations for his service in Vietnam,
discharged from the Air Force in 1975.[1]

Homosexuals have served in America's military since the Revolutionary War, often heroically. Although homosexuality in the armed forces was not condoned, and many homosexuals were forced out of service because of their sexuality, homosexual activity was not formally treated as a crime by the military until early in the twentieth century. During World War I, the Articles of War as amended in 1919 made sodomy a felony. Many homosexual servicemen were sent to prison as criminals in the 1920s and 1930s.[2]

As the U.S. armed services undertook their massive mobilization for World War II, the way the military viewed

Sergeant Leonard Matlovich received an honorable discharge from the Air Force after exhausting legal avenues to remain in the service and openly gay.

and treated homosexuality changed (as it was changing outside the military) from crime to mental illness. Homosexuals were still banned from military service.

Nonetheless, many did serve, despite being at constant risk for being kicked out of the armed forces with less than honorable discharges—a permanent blot on one's record that makes landing a civilian job much more difficult. Enforcement of the ban on homosexuals has always been selective, depending largely on the whim of specific military commanders and on how badly the armed forces need troops. During World War II, the Korean War, and especially the Vietnam War and the subsequent transition from the draft to an all-volunteer force, discharges for homosexuality plummeted.

The early gay liberationists were generally aligned with the anti-Vietnam War movement of the late 1960s and early 1970s. For many years discrimination against homosexuals who wanted to serve in the military was a low priority for the gay rights movement. Although a few individuals accused by the military of homosexuality in the 1970s and 1980s fought their discharges (sometimes with assistance from the American Civil Liberties Union), most accepted their fate and left the armed forces quietly.

In 1981 the Pentagon codified its policy on gays in the military in a brief statement that remained in effect for more than a decade:

> Homosexuality is incompatible with military service. The presence in the military environment of persons who engage in homosexual conduct or who, by their statements, demonstrate a propensity to engage in homosexual conduct, seriously impairs the accomplishment of military mission. The presence of such members adversely affects the ability of the military services to maintain

discipline, good order and morale; to foster mutual trust and confidence among service members; to insure the integrity of the system of rank and command; to facilitate assignment and worldwide deployment of service members who frequently must live and work under close conditions affording minimal privacy; to recruit and retain members of the military services; to maintain the public acceptability of military service; and to prevent breaches of security."[3]

Thousands of service men and women were accused of homosexuality and discharged from the military in the 1980s. Lesbians were especially hard hit: The percentage of those discharged for homosexuality who were women was consistently much higher than the overall percentage of service members who were women. (The proportion of servicewomen who were lesbians was apparently actually *decreasing* in the 1980s as military service became a more socially acceptable and attractive choice for heterosexual women.) *All* women in the armed forces were affected: Sexual harassment was common as more and more women were integrated into the traditionally male-dominated military, and women who complained about harassment were often accused of being lesbians.

Gay military men at the same time faced a different problem—AIDS. In the early 1980s, an AIDS diagnosis often triggered a homosexuality discharge—without medical benefits. (A more humane policy took effect in 1987, and the military has since treated AIDS among service members more like other diseases.)

As AIDS vividly demonstrated, the U.S. armed forces are not isolated from the rest of America. Outside and inside the military in the 1980s, gay men and lesbians were becoming much more open about their sexual orientation.

As in the past, in the 1980s only a fraction of homosexual service members were discharged. Those who stayed in found that increasing numbers of their comrades and commanders privately thought that the gay ban was foolish for several reasons: Gay soldiers could do their jobs just fine (and were allowed to serve openly in the armed forces of most U.S. allies). The military needed all the good soldiers it could get, and it couldn't afford to discharge expensively trained, skilled, and willing troops. (The annual cost associated with homosexuality discharges in the 1980s has been variously estimated at tens to hundreds of millions of dollars.)

Those homosexual service members who stayed in also discovered, unfortunately, that many service members hated homosexuality and would inform on them to military investigators—or even attack them violently. Like the women who were victims of sexual harassment and assault, male victims of beatings and other violent gay bashing often just put up with it rather than complain and risk a homosexuality discharge.[4]

Policy Changes in the Clinton Administration

During the presidential election campaign of 1992, candidate Bill Clinton promised to end the ban on gays in the military should he become president. Although his promise attracted little attention during the campaign, a storm of controversy swept Washington very early in his administration, in January 1993, about whether and how such a policy change might be implemented. Congress was flooded with telephone calls made at the urging of religious right organizations opposed to ending the ban. General Colin Powell, widely popular and the first African American to be chairman of the Joint Chiefs of Staff, defended the ban and insisted that integrating gays

In November 1993, former senator Barry Goldwater discussed his views on gays in the military, among other things, on "The Tonight Show with Jay Leno."

Conservative icon Barry Goldwater, a former senator and Republican presidential candidate and a lifelong advocate for a strong U.S. military, spoke out in 1993 in favor of gays in the military:

"After more than fifty years in the military and politics, I am still amazed to see how upset people can get over nothing. Lifting the ban on gays in the military isn't exactly nothing, but it's pretty damned close.

"Everyone knows that gays have served honorably in the military since at least the time of Julius Caesar. They'll still be serving long after we're all dead and buried. That should not surprise anyone.

"But most Americans should be shocked to know that...the military has wasted a half-billion dollars over the past decade chasing down gays and running them out of the armed services....

"I served in the armed forces. I have flown more than 150 of the best fighter planes and bombers this country manufactured. I founded the Arizona National Guard. I chaired the Senate Armed Services Committee. And I think it's high time to pull the curtains on this charade of policy....

"Under our Constitution, everyone is guaranteed the right to do as he pleases as long as it does not harm someone else. You don't need to be 'straight' to fight and die for your country. You just need to shoot straight."[5]

into the military was not at all the same as integrating blacks into the military—a highly controversial measure when it was undertaken after World War II.

In late January, President Clinton backed away from his promise to end the ban with a "stroke of a pen." He announced that he would refrain for six months from issuing an executive order ending the ban.

After a prolonged tussle with Pentagon officials and members of Congress who favored continuing the ban, the White House announced a compromise. Under the compromise, the U.S. military would no longer ask recruits about their sexual orientation. Homosexual

Gay World War II veterans in front of the White House during the March on Washington for Gay and Lesbian Rights in April 1993.

Don't Ask, Don't Tell, Don't Pursue

Date: July 19, 1993
Subject: Policy on Homosexual Conduct in the Armed Forces....

"The Department of Defense has long held that, as a general rule, homosexuality is incompatible with military service because it interferes with the factors critical to combat effectiveness, including unit morale, unit cohesiveness, and individual privacy. Nevertheless, the Department of Defense also recognizes that individuals with a homosexual orientation have served with distinction in the armed services of the United States.

"Therefore, it is the policy of the Department of Defense to judge the suitability of persons to serve in the armed forces on the basis of their conduct. Homosexual conduct will be grounds for separation from the military services. Sexual orientation is considered a personal and private matter, and homosexual orientation is not a bar to service entry or continued service unless manifested by homosexual conduct.

"I direct the following:

"Applicants for military service will not be asked or required to reveal their sexual orientation. Applicants will be informed of accession and separation policy.

"Service members will be separated [from military service] for homosexual conduct.

"Commanders and investigating agencies will not initiate inquiries or investigations solely to determine a member's sexual orientation. Service members will not be asked or required to reveal their sexual orientation. However, commanders will continue to initiate inquiries or investigations, as appropriate, when there is credible information that a basis for discharge or disciplinary action exists."

—Memorandum by Secretary of Defense Les Aspin[6]

behavior still would be grounds for dismissal, but unpublicized homosexual orientation by itself would not. The military was not to investigate sexual orientation, but would continue to investigate charges of forbidden conduct, including homosexual sex.

The new policy, known as "don't ask, don't tell, don't pursue," took effect in February 1994. Despite several challenges in court, it remained in effect as of early 2000.

Even under "don't ask, don't tell," the military continued to pursue cases characterized by homosexual orientation rather than conduct. For example, in 1997 the Navy aggressively dug up sexual orientation information about Timothy R. McVeigh, a chief petty officer with seventeen years of unblemished service—even persuading his Internet service provider to reveal information about his private e-mail—and sought his discharge. (After a legal battle, McVeigh was allowed to retire with full benefits and payment of his legal fees.)[7]

The number of service members discharged for homosexuality actually rose each year after "don't ask, don't tell" went into effect. In 1998, according to Pentagon statistics, 1,145 service members were discharged for homosexuality—up 13 percent from 1997 and nearly double the number in 1993, the year before the new policy took effect.[8] The military attributed the rise to an increase in "statement" cases—individuals openly declaring their homosexuality either to get out of the military or to make a political point. Gay rights activists attributed it to persistent efforts by military brass to undermine the policy and continue to pursue homosexuals. In December 1999, President Clinton criticized how the policy had been implemented. In early 2000, both Democratic presidential candidates asserted that gays should be allowed to serve openly.

Gays in the Church

"Your problem is not a chemical imbalance. It's not hered-
itary. Your problem is the lifestyle which you have chosen.
And every Christian community has a pastor who can help
you change your lifestyle."

—Ira A. Edens, a South Carolina conservative
Republican, on gay activists.[1]

While America is home to a kaleidoscope of religious
variety, it is predominantly Christian—and organized
opposition to gay rights has been overwhelmingly dominated by conservative Christians. For this reason, this
chapter begins with a close look at Jewish and Christian
scriptures concerning homosexuality, before moving on
to the place of gay men and lesbians in American
churches.

Scripture and Homosexuality

Interpretations of scriptures
regarding homosexuality have
been as diverse as the personal
histories, religious affiliations, and political agendas of

the individuals who believe in them. Only a handful of Bible passages address or allude to homosexuality. All are discussed in the next few paragraphs.

The Bible story most often cited concerning homosexuality is that of the city of Sodom. In Genesis 19, a man named Lot invited two strangers (angels in disguise) to stay overnight at his house in Sodom. After dinner, "the men of Sodom, both young and old, all the people to the last man, surrounded the house; and they called to Lot, 'Where are the men who came to you tonight? Bring them out to us, that we may know them.'" Lot begged the Sodomites not to "act so wickedly," but they persisted. The angels struck the men blind, and in the morning God destroyed the entire city. (A similar story is told in Judges 19–20, and in the New Testament. II Peter 2:6 and Jude 7 both refer to God's punishment of Sodom.)[2]

Conservative American Christians have primarily interpreted this story as God punishing the Sodomites for homosexuality. Others, however, point out that the story makes more sense if the primary sin is inhospitality: that Lot was not a native of Sodom and his guests were likely suspected of spying, that the ancient word translated as "know" is ambiguous, and that the Sodomites likely wanted to interrogate and perhaps execute Lot's guests. Even if homosexuality was involved, these revisionists argue, what they wanted to do was rape the strangers, and rape is immoral whether it's a man raping a man or a man raping a woman.

Apparently less ambiguous are Leviticus 18:22 ("You shall not lie with a male as with a woman; it is an abomination.") and Leviticus 20:13 ("If a man lies with a male as with a woman, both of them have committed an abomination; they shall be put to death, their blood is upon them.") The predominant Jewish and Christian interpretation of these passages is that homosexuality is a serious sin. Some revisionists argue, however, that these verses

This lithograph depicts Lot and his family fleeing Sodom.

refer either specifically to male prostitutes associated with idol-worshiping cults or to ritual uncleanness (a condition that also occurs if, for example, a man touches a corpse or a menstruating woman) rather than immoral behavior.

In the New Testament, the Apostle Paul in Romans 1:26-27 says: "For this reason God gave them [those who do not honor him] up to dishonorable passions. Their women exchanged natural relations for the unnatural, and the men likewise gave up natural relations with women, and were consumed with passion for one another, men committing shameful acts with men and receiving in their own persons the due penalty for their error." Conservative Christians once again read this as a clear-cut condemnation of homosexuality. Revisionists note that Paul likely had in mind prostitutes and men who had sex with young boys (relations that, like rape, are immoral regardless of the sex of the individuals involved). Another revisionist interpretation sees this as a description of presumably heterosexual people acting against their God-given nature; in this view, for homosexuals to reject their God-given homosexual nature would be just as sinful.

Paul also apparently includes homosexuality in a list of sins in I Corinthians 6:9–10 ("Do you know that the unrighteous will not inherit the kingdom of God? Do not be deceived; neither the immoral, nor idolators, nor adulterers, nor homosexuals, nor thieves, nor the greedy, nor drunkards, nor revilers, nor robbers will inherit the kingdom of God.") and I Timothy 1:9–10 ("the law is not laid down for the just but for the lawless and sinners, for the unholy and profane, for murderers of fathers and murderers of mothers, for manslayers, immoral persons, sodomites, kidnappers, liars, perjurers"). Revisionists, however, note that the true meaning of the ancient words translated here as "homosexuals" and "sodomites" is unclear; they might instead mean "prostitutes," "pederasts," or "masturbators."

Overall, those who believe that homosexuality is a sin typically also believe that it is a choice—something you choose to do (like rape or adultery), rather than something you are (an inherent characteristic like race or eye color). Similarly, those who believe that homosexual sex isn't necessarily sinful generally believe that homosexuality is an inherent characteristic, that God created gay people and loves them as they are.

Here, from a conservative Christian writer and teacher, is a summary of his very typical argument against homosexuality:

1. Scripture must be the primary and final authority for sexual morality....

2. Homosexual acts...depart from the only acceptable avenue for the full expression of sexuality, which is heterosexual marriage....

3. Homosexual acts constitute a negation of marriage, not merely a variant expression of sexuality....

4. Homosexual practice involves a high probability of harmful associated phenomena: promiscuity, substance abuse, depression, suicide, and pedophilia....

5. Male homosexual acts involve practices that are injurious to the body and that involve a high risk of infectious disease....

6. While a homosexual orientation is probably caused for each individual by several factors in combination, at the level of action each person is morally accountable....

7. Change is possible.... Christian faith and Christian community...offer unique and powerful supports to people in transition [from a homosexual to a heterosexual orientation].[3]

Gays in the Church

American religious organizations are diverse, and so have been their attitudes toward homosexuality:

- Orthodox Judaism flatly forbids homosexuality. (So do Mormonism and orthodox Islam.)

However, the Reform Judaism movement (which represents the largest number of American Jews) has endorsed civil rights protections for homosexuals and has ordained openly gay and lesbian rabbis. Some Reform congregations have been especially welcoming of gay men and lesbians, and some Reform rabbis have performed same-sex commitment ceremonies.

- The Catholic Church since 1986 has held that homosexual orientation is not in itself sinful, but that all homosexual behavior is. Priests and nuns have been suspended from their duties or even expelled from their orders for ministering to homosexuals in ways that the church has found too approving of homosexual behavior.

- Some bishops of the Episcopal Church (the American branch of the Anglican Church) have ordained openly gay and lesbian priests and deacons, and some Episcopal priests have blessed same-sex unions. Anglican leadership outside the United States has been much less liberal where homosexuality is concerned: In August 1998 an international conference of Anglican bishops voted 526–70 for a resolution stating that "homosexual practice is incompatible with Scripture," advising against allowing homosexuals to become priests, and opposing same-sex marriage.[4]

- Among Protestants, the more liberal denominations have been more accommodating of homosexuality. Quakers and Unitarians, for example, have accepted and supported stable and committed gay relationships for decades.

- Conservative Protestant denominations, most notably the Southern Baptists, have not only

At this Lutheran ordination ceremony in January 1990, the congregation is placing their hands on the new ministers, two lesbians and a gay man. The ordinations defy the Lutheran Church of America's national laws.

ORTHODOX JUDAISM AND HOMOSEXUALITY

"I am an Orthodox rabbi and I am gay. For a long while I denied, rejected, railed against this truth. The life story that I had wanted—wife, kids, and a family that modeled Torah [Jewish scripture] and hesed [steadfast love/loyalty]—turned out to be an impossible fantasy. I have begun to shape a new life story....

"God can only require the doable.... Gay people cannot be asked to be straight, but they can be asked to 'hold fast to the covenant' [the contract between God and his people]....

"Holding fast to the covenant demands that I fulfill the mitzvot [religious obligations] that are in my power to fulfill. I cannot marry and bear children, but there are other ways to build a family....

"Holding fast to the covenant demands that I seek a path toward sanctity in gay sexual life. The Torah has much to say about the way people create kedusha [holiness] in their sexual relationships. The values of marriage, monogamy, modesty, and faithfulness which are central to the [Jewish] tradition's view of holiness need to be applied in ways that shape choices and lifestyles....

"There are myriad Jewish concerns, moral, social, intellectual, and spiritual, that I cannot abandon. Being gay need not overwhelm the rest of Jewish life."[5]

strongly condemned homosexuality as sinful but also spearheaded antigay rights political actions in the United States in the 1970s, 1980s, and 1990s. In 1988 the Southern Baptist Convention labeled homosexual behavior "an abomination, a perversion, and the manifestation of a depraved nature."[6]

THE CATHOLIC CHURCH ON HOMOSEXUALITY

"Although the particular inclination of the homo-sexual person is not a sin, it is a more or less strong tendency ordered toward an intrinsic moral evil; and thus the inclination itself must be seen as an objective disorder.

"Therefore, special concern and pastoral attention should be directed toward those who have this condition, lest they be led to believe that the living out of this orientation in homosexual activity is a morally acceptable option. It is not....

"The Church, obedient to the Lord who founded her and gave to her the sacramental life, celebrates the divine plan of the loving and life-giving union of men and women in the sacrament of marriage. It is only in the marital relationship that the use of the sexual faculty can be morally good. A person engaging in homosexual behavior therefore acts immorally.

"To choose someone of the same sex for one's sexual activity is to annul the rich symbolism and meaning, not to mention the goals, of the Creator's sexual design. Homosexual activity is not a comple-mentary union, able to transmit life; and so it thwarts the call to a life of that form of self-giving which the Gospel says is the essence of Christian living. This does not mean that homosexual persons are not often generous and giving of themselves; but when they engage in homosexual activity they confirm within themselves a disordered sexual incli-nation which is essentially self-indulgent.

"As in every moral disorder, homosexual activity prevents one's own fulfillment and happiness by acting contrary to the creative wisdom of God....

"What, then, are homosexual persons to do who seek to follow the Lord? Fundamentally, they are called to enact the will of God in their life by

> joining whatever sufferings and difficulties they experience in virtue of their condition to the sacrifice of the Lord's Cross....
>
> "Christians who are homosexual are called, as all of us are, to a chaste life."
>
> —Joseph Cardinal Ratzinger, 1986, "Letter to the Bishops of the Catholic Church on the Pastoral Care of Homosexual Persons"[7]

- Even among conservative and middle-of-the-road denominations, many local churches and individual clergy have been more liberal and accepting toward homosexuals than their national governing bodies. For example, a local Baptist church in North Carolina attracted national attention in 1998 when its members gave its ministers permission to bless "all loving, committed and exclusive relationships between two people"— including same-sex relationships.[8]

Opposition to gay rights in particular and homosexuality in general has been a prominent, persistent, and highly emotional fund-raising appeal for such religious right organizations as Moral Majority, the Christian Coalition, and Focus on the Family. In an early example, a 1981 fund-raising letter, Moral Majority founder Jerry Falwell wrote: "Please remember, homosexuals do not reproduce! They recruit! And, many of them are out after my children and your children."[9] Liberal Christian and secular critics of such pumped-up rhetoric contend not only that it's inaccurate but also (in their own emotional appeal) that it can only be described as un-Christian hate propaganda akin to the ugliest outpourings of the Ku Klux Klan and other bigots.

The Lutheran Church started expulsion proceedings against ministers Phyllis Zillhart and Ruth Frost, shown here in 1993, because of their openly lesbian relationship.

A GAY CHRISTIAN MINISTER

"I believe...that each of us, gay and nongay alike, is called by our Creator to accept our sexual orientation as a gift; and that we are called to exercise that gift with integrity, creativity, and responsibility.... Homosexuality is not something you change or heal or overcome.

"[Leaders of the religious right have] all lied when they talked about a corrupt gay and lesbian lifestyle, as though there were one lifestyle for all lesbians and gays. In fact, we are church organists and choir directors, deacons and members of the board, pastors, priests, and rabbis. We pray to the same God. We read the same Scriptures. We are responsible parents, pastors, teachers, and lay leaders. Gay people are at the core, not at the fringe, of this great nation....

"The religious right is wrong: wrong about the Bible, wrong about Jesus, wrong about God, wrong about the church, wrong about the family, and seriously wrong about gay and lesbian people....

"I know personally what it means to be a victim of this uninformed and noncompassionate 'Christian' position on homosexuality. I went through 25 years of Christian counseling and 'ex-gay therapy' including electric shock to try to overcome my sexual and affectional orientation. Finally, feeling abandoned by God, by the church, and by society, I longed to end my life....

"The Bible makes it clear. Doing justice...is the work of God. When we see an individual or a group...being treated unfairly, Jesus calls us to do something to help end the suffering....

"Doing justice begins by walking away from the churches and the synagogues, the preachers, priests, and rabbis, who use God's word to condemn us and into churches and fellowships where we are loved and respected as God's children who happen to be lesbian or gay. It begins by withholding our tithes and offerings from homophobic churches...and by giving our money and volunteering our time to churches...that are working for justice...by preaching and teaching justice in our own churches and synagogues; by organizing and training our congregations to do some justice and not just to talk about it;...by fighting for justice wherever and however we can on behalf of all our fellow Americans who suffer....

"When we act in faith, there is enough light in this world to conquer the darkness."

—Mel White, dean of a large gay-friendly Christian church and former ghostwriter for leaders of the religious right[10]

Beyond the political arena, gay men and lesbians of nearly every denomination in America have formed groups that provide fellowship and seek to reconcile homosexuality with their religious traditions. Some of these groups have been embraced by their churches' leadership, some (like the Catholic group Dignity) maintain an uneasy coexistence, and some have been "exiled" from their parent churches.

Finally, there are independent churches specifically dedicated to ministering to gay men and lesbians. The best known of these, Metropolitan Community Churches, grew out of a Christian ministry founded by the Reverend Troy Perry in 1968. It now includes more than three hundred congregations worldwide.[11]

Gay Marriage and Family Life

"The two-parent family—a man and woman united in marriage—is the best environment in which to raise children. Public policy should uphold the two-parent family."

—Family Research Council[1]

While growing numbers of gay and lesbian couples have taken marriage vows in religious and other commitment ceremonies, these are not recognized as valid marriages by any state in the United States. Gay activists in the 1990s have aggressively sought for gay and lesbian couples the right to legally marry and to adopt children and retain custody and visitation rights. Antigay activists have fiercely opposed them.

Gay Marriage

Some conservative Christians and Jews have focused less on what homosexuality is (a sin, in their view) and more on what it isn't: heterosexual marriage. They say that heterosexual marriage with children is God's model for how humans should live their lives and the only context in which sex is holy, and that scripture is essentially a blueprint for how to live that (married) life. Homosexuality, they say, simply has no place in God's plan for us—and gay "marriage" isn't marriage at all.

Religious homosexuals, on the other hand, note that same-sex marriages can, and in many cases do, foster most or all of the virtues that any godly marriage should: love, commitment, taking care of family, aiding the community, even raising children.

In the United States, marriage is both a religious experience and a legal, civil contract. Many churches in recent years have blessed the unions of homosexual members. The gay-oriented Universal Fellowship of Metropolitan Community Churches has been conducting same-sex "Holy Union" ceremonies since 1968—more than two thousand each year by the mid-1990s.[2] Many liberal Protestant churches have blessed such unions, and even the denominations most opposed to homosexuality have seen such unions blessed by a few of their clergy. In addition, many couples have devised nonreligious commitment ceremonies in which both partners pledge to love, honor, and take care of one another.

But meaningful as each of these same-sex ceremonies has been to its participants, not one has been legally binding anywhere in the United States. Ironically, churches, which typically do impose qualification-related requirements on those they will marry (classes, counseling, confessions of faith), have been more willing to marry homosexual couples than the state, which treats marriage as a fundamental civil right and imposes no such requirements.

Legal marriage brings with it serious obligations—and significant benefits, such as spousal health insurance benefits, shared pension rights, tax advantages, various

Above: Two men exchange vows and rings during their religious "Holy Union" ceremony at Metropolitan Community Church in Los Angeles in 1972.

Right: Antigay protesters from Westboro Baptist Church in Topeka, Kansas, traveled to Broadway United Methodist Church in Chicago in 1998 to protest a ceremony uniting two gay men.

Passed by Congress and signed into law in 1996, the Defense of Marriage Act specifies:

"Powers Reserved to the States... No State, territory, or possession of the United States, or Indian tribe, shall be required to give effect to any public act, record, or judicial proceeding of any other State, territory, possession, or tribe respecting a relationship between persons of the same sex that is treated as a marriage under the laws of such other State, territory, possession, or tribe, or a right or claim arising from such relationship....

"Definition of Marriage... In determining the meaning of any Act of Congress, or of any ruling, regulation, or interpretation of the various administrative bureaus and agencies of the United States, the word 'marriage' means only a legal union between one man and one woman as husband and wife, and the word 'spouse' refers only to a person of the opposite sex who is a husband or wife."[3]

inheritance rights, and family rates on everything from swimming pool passes to auto insurance. It also carries the intangible but very important benefit of conveying to the world that the two people involved are truly family.

Unable to be legally married, same-sex couples pursuing a committed relationship must (with the often expensive help of lawyers and accountants) painstakingly piece together a mosaic of protections and sharing arrangements that are either automatic or far simpler for legally married couples, from wills to joint property ownership to name changes. Although many corporations and some local governments have extended spousal benefits to the unmarried domestic partners (gay and straight) of their employees, some protections and benefits are simply unavailable to gay couples.

Antigay activists believe that this is as it should be, that marriage should be reserved for heterosexual couples because God intended it to be that way and because society has an interest in encouraging stable, traditional, child-bearing families.

Gay rights activists counter that marriage is a civil right as well as a religious sacrament, and that all they are asking for is the same legal status currently available to atheists and sterile couples as well as religiously observant, child-bearing heterosexuals. In addition, many have observed that society's interest in stable families would be furthered still more by encouraging stable homosexual families as well as traditional heterosexual ones. "Given the fact that we already allow legal gay relationships," gay Catholic conservative Andrew Sullivan writes: "what possible social goal is advanced by framing the law to encourage those relationships to be unfaithful, undeveloped, and insecure?"[4]

In 1993 gay marriage became a subject of much national debate when Hawaii's Supreme Court reversed a lower court ban on same-sex marriages, saying that if the state wishes to ban such marriages it must prove a "compelling public interest."[5] (The case began when three gay couples applied for marriage licenses in 1990.) The court's action didn't actually legalize gay marriage in Hawaii, but it did force the state and antigay marriage activists to justify their position in court and before Hawaii's voters.

The Hawaii court action also spurred antigay rights activists to introduce explicit bans on same-sex marriages in state legislatures and through voter referendums across the country. At the national level, Congress debated and passed the Defense of Marriage Act, which

Ray Boylan and his partner, Stanley Wilson, invited family and friends to witness their commitment ceremony in 1996. Formerly a doctor and a dentist, they now run an inn together.

"We felt it was really important for our families to understand our seriousness," Boylan says, "that we aren't just promiscuous party boys. We, like other people, feel that a ceremony gives others a familiar context for understanding what's happening right before their eyes. How else would Stanley ever agree to kiss me in front of his mother?

"Having our friends there was mainly a staging thing—it helped us to feel supported and comforted. All those smiling faces—even if we didn't have a ceremony, just having that many wonderful people from so many places and times in one room would have to be almost magical.

"It was also a chance to have a really great party. Just picking the menu was lots of fun. And we got new suits.

"Everyone at work already knew that I was gay. But making some of them come to this (they couldn't refuse!) was a treat just in itself.

"Yes, we would get married legally if we could. In actuality, with a good lawyer and a little foresight, one can plan for wills and property and money quite well without marriage. For other things, like insurance, being married is a benefit. And for couples where one partner is not an American citizen, it is a true human rights issue that gays are not marriageable—partners risk deportation after having to jump through innumerable hurdles over visa issues.

"Like any couple we negotiate our issues and deal with our conflicts. But it's a comfort knowing we've been committed—we have witnesses."[6]

was signed into law by President Clinton in September 1996. This law forbade federal recognition and federal tax and pension benefits for same-sex marriage partners and gave states the right to refuse to recognize any same-sex marriages that might be performed in other states.

By December 1999, thirty states had adopted laws banning same-sex marriage—including Hawaii.[7] In November 1998 voters in Hawaii and Alaska passed statewide measures banning gay marriage.

After these votes, the focus for activists interested in gay marriage shifted to Vermont. In mid-November 1998, that state's Supreme Court began hearing the case of three couples (two gay men and four lesbians) who were suing the state for the right to marry. In December 1999, the court unanimously ruled tht the state must grant gay and lesbian couples the same protections and benefits as heterosexual couples, either by allowing gay marriage or by creating an equivalent domestic parnership option. The Vermont legislature was expected to debate the matter in 2000.

Gay Parenting

Gay men and lesbians have often had children in heterosexual marriages before acknowledging their homosexuality; many of these children have subsequently been raised in part or entirely by one parent and his or her same-sex partner. (One strong argument for same-sex marriage is to extend to these children the same benefits and protections enjoyed by the children of remarried heterosexual couples.) In addition, lesbians have long used artificial insemination to become pregnant and bear and raise children. In some cases, mixed groups of gay men and lesbians have collaborated on conceiving and raising children. Recently, a small number of gay men have hired surrogates to become pregnant through artificial insemi-

Two mothers with their sixteen-month-old son

nation and bear a child so that they can raise children to whom they are biologically related.[8]

All of these arrangements are anathema to antigay activists, who believe that children need heterosexual parents as role models. Nonetheless, the religious right strongly supports parents' rights to raise their children as they see fit and so has not generally sought to restrict the parental rights of gay biological parents.

Custody disputes and adoption are another story. Antigay activists generally encourage courts to consider homosexuality a strong negative that a gay or lesbian parent has to overcome to win custody or the right to visit his or her children. In states where sodomy is illegal, homosexuals have in some cases been treated as presumptive criminals and thus unfit parents for their children. In 1993, for example, a Virginia court gave custody of a two-year-old to his grandmother, taking him away from his lesbian mother on these grounds.[9]

In the past, adoption authorities have often been hostile to homosexuals. However, quietly, and typically in the absence of any overall policy directives, state and local courts across the country in recent years have allowed increasing numbers of single-parent, stepparent, and joint adoptions by homosexuals. Religious right activists have decried this trend. "It seems to have government saying that a gay environment is a good one to grow up in," a spokeswoman for the Christian-right Family Research Council explains.[10]

The courts may see it differently. "Courts are more used to having to coerce people to take responsibility for and care for their children," a gay rights activist notes, "and so when someone, anyone comes in asking to be made responsible, they are very sympathetic."[11]

As of mid-1999, only one state, Florida, refused categorically to allow joint adoptions by same-sex couples. Most other states, however, made it more difficult for anyone other than married heterosexuals to adopt a child. Many states, for example, required two separate adoption proceedings (one for each parent), a lengthy and expensive process.[12]

Activists' Voices

In this chapter, activists on both sides of the gay rights controversy explain, in their own words, who they are, what they do, and where they stand. Gay rights is only one among many "family values" issues with which the four "anti" organizations profiled below are concerned— but it has figured very prominently in their literature, especially their fund-raising appeals. Similarly, the four pro-gay organizations covered here concern themselves with other issues as well, from AIDS to education to (in the case of the ACLU) a broad defense of civil liberties in general.

Antihomosexual Activists

Founded in 1989 by religious right television evangelist Pat Robertson after his failed run for the Republican presidential nomination in 1988, the Christian Coalition by late 1998 claimed "approximately 1.9 million members and supporters nationwide, with nearly 2,000 chapters formed in all fifty states." The Christian Coalition's leadership in Chesapeake, Virginia, and its local chapters "train activists, engage in voter registration drives, distribute voter guides, activate community policy networks, and build relationships with church liaisons and neighborhood coordinators."

Outgoing Christian Coalition president Ralph Reed (left) talks with Pat Robertson. The Christian Coalition had 400,000 dues-paying members when this photo was taken in 1997.

In February 1998, after claiming credit for the defeat of a statewide gay rights measure in Maine, the Christian Coalition's national leadership announced "Families 2000, a strategy to place family issues at the forefront in the next two election cycles and into the new century...[that] seeks to recruit 100,000 'church liaisons' by November 2000...[who] will represent their churches in our local Christian Coalition chapters....

"The Families 2000 strategy includes a menu of issues for state and local action.... The issues include...repeal of legislation giving special rights based on sexual behavior [and] defeat of state gay-adoption laws.

"Along with Families 2000, Christian Coalition's long term goal is to identify 10 million pro-family voters and have neighborhood coordinators in each of America's 175,000 precincts. Clearly, Christian Coalition expects to have a permanent impact on American public policy." [2]

In June 1999, press reports disclosed that the Christian Coalition, long accused of favoring Republican over Democratic candidates in its voter guides, had lost its tax-exempt nonprofit status with the Internal Revenue Service. The organization responded by splitting itself into two groups, one political and the other nonprofit. Saddled with a $2.5 million debt, deflated membership, and high turnover in its leadership at all levels, the Christian Coalition had a long way to go to regain its former clout.[3]

Focus on the Family is a Christian media ministry based in Colorado and led by Dr. James C. Dobson. In addition to its extensive radio and TV broadcasting, it publishes a wide array of books, pamphlets, and other materials focusing on "helping to preserve traditional values and the institution of the family."

James Dobson, founder of Focus on the Family, holds up a Bible as he speaks at a convention.

Among its statements of "who we are and what we stand for" is the following text headed "Heterosexuality and Homosexuality":

"Since the heart of God's plan for the family is the marriage of a man and a woman, and since families are the basic building blocks of society, then it follows that societies will only be as strong as the relationships between men and women. Heterosexuality is fundamental to the vitality and even the existence of any society.

"Scripture is very clear in its condemnation of homosexual conduct, for such sin is a deviation from God's creation and design... Focus on the Family calls all Christians to sincerely love and understand those involved in the homosexual life... Homosexuals are entitled to the same basic rights as other citizens.

"Nevertheless, Focus does take strong exception to the activist movement that seeks to gain special privileges and protected minority status for the homosexual community. There is no evidence that homosexuals as a class are discriminated against in the present society. They are not like African-Americans, Hispanics or other historically disadvantaged groups, for they have far higher average incomes and education than most Americans, along with a significant political influence.

"Focus on the Family also opposes the efforts of radical homosexual 'social reformers' who wish to redefine the family, permit homosexual 'marriages,' be able to adopt children and recruit the young. This and other elements of the more radical homosexual agenda must be vigorously opposed.

"Further, there is no established scientific evidence that sexual orientation is genetically determined by brain structure.... Moral choice is real, and it is central to our identity as men and women.

"The sin of homosexual behavior, like all sins, can be forgiven and healed by the grace revealed in the life and death of Christ.... Focus on the Family has seen that, by God's grace and through compassionate counseling, it is sometimes possible, although always difficult, for a person to move from a homosexual to a heterosexual orientation.

"When that change appears impossible in an individual case, such a person is in the same position as the heterosexual single who has no prospects of marriage. They are both called by Scripture to a life of sexual abstinence."[4]

Family Research Council (FRC) has been closely associated with Focus on the Family. (From 1988 to 1992 they were merged.) Until early 1999, when he launched his campaign for the Republican presidential nomination in 2000, FRC was led by Gary Bauer, an often-interviewed commentator on the politics of "family values" issues. FRC is based in Washington, D.C.

In its own words, "Family Research Council's primary reason for existence is to reaffirm and promote nationally and particularly in Washington, D.C., the traditional family and the Judeo-Christian principles upon which it is built.... FRC's commitment is to work as an advocate for the family to the legislative, executive, and judicial branches of the federal government."

"FRC on the Issues" includes the following gay rights related points:

"Definition of 'Family.' The Family Research Council agrees with the U.S. Census Bureau's definition that a 'family' is a group of people living together in the same household who are related to one another by blood, marriage, and/or adoption."

"Family Structure. The two-parent family—a man and woman united in marriage—is the best environment in which to raise children. Public policy should uphold the two-parent family."

"Homosexuality. The Family Research Council believes that homosexuality is unhealthy, immoral, and destructive to individuals, families and societies. Compassion—not bigotry—impels us to support healing for homosexuals who want to change their sexual preference. FRC opposes any attempts to equate homosexuality with benign characteristics such as skin color or place of origin and to teach children that it is normal and desirable behavior."

"Homosexuals in the Military. The Family Research Council opposes the induction of homosexuals into the military because their known presence destroys morale and sexual privacy and introduces sexual tension into the

Gary Bauer participates in a radio talk show.

barracks. FRC opposes attempts to subvert the law barring anyone with homosexual 'propensities' from military service."[5]

In a newspaper opinion piece, Gary Bauer has written that gay rights activists "say they want civil rights enjoyed by all Americans (which they already have). But they really want special rights....

"Homosexual activists want to use the power of law to force acceptance of behaviors that destroy family life and individuals. Already the Boy Scouts are under attack in several 'gay rights' states for adhering to time-tested morality in guiding boys toward manhood. The scouts are deemed a 'hate' organization. So, too, are churches that won't ordain homosexual ministers. America's armed forces are condemned for putting military readiness before individual idiosyncrasies.... Many college campuses now endorse homosexuality and punish those who believe otherwise....

"It is understandable that many people are moved by pleas for 'tolerance' and 'justice.' But the gay rights movement is not about either. It is about harnessing government power....

"No culture in history has cut the bonds of sexual restraint and devalued marriage and family—and survived."[6]

Most prominent among the controversial "ex-gay" organizations (see Chapter 7) has been Exodus International. According to Exodus's own description of itself, "For over twenty years, Exodus has been proclaiming freedom from homosexuality by offering support, instruction, and compassion for those who desire to change....

"Each journey [out of homosexuality] begins with a personal commitment to God and His created intent for human sexuality. Through a recovery process, each struggler can learn to 'walk out' of homosexuality by developing trust and obedience in Jesus and His victory over all sin.

"In time, the specific hurts and emotional deficits which helped lay a foundation for homosexual desires can be addressed through insight, personal action, and the power of the Holy Spirit. The struggler can then move into greater maturity and wholeness by cooperating with God, which allows the freedom to grow into heterosexuality....

"Exodus is a nonprofit, nondenominational organization. Its mission is to equip and unite Christian agencies and individuals to effectively communicate the message

"If there were no alternative to today's conflicted politics of homosexuality, we might be condemned to see [activists] fight noisily while society stumbles from one awkward compromise to another. But there is an alternative: a politics that can reconcile the best arguments of liberals and conservatives, and find a way to marry the two....

"This politics affirms a simple and limited principle: that all public (as opposed to private) discrimination against homosexuals be ended and that every right and responsibility that heterosexuals enjoy as public citizens be extended to those who grow up and find themselves different. And that is all....

"What would it mean in practice? Quite simply, an end to all proactive discrimination by the state against homosexuals. That means an end to sodomy laws that apply only to homosexuals; a recourse to the courts if there is not equal protection of heterosexuals and homosexuals in law enforcement; an equal legal age of consent to sexual activity for heterosexuals and homosexuals;... inclusion of the facts about homosexuality in the curriculum of every government-funded school;... recourse to the courts if any government body or agency can be proven to be engaged in discrimination against homosexual employees; equal opportunity and inclusion in the military; and legal homosexual marriage and divorce....

"These [last two] measures—ending the military ban and lifting the marriage bar—are simple, direct, and require no change in heterosexual behavior and no sacrifice from heterosexuals. They represent a politics that tackles the heart of prejudice against homosexuals while leaving bigots their

of liberation from homosexuality, as well as support individuals facing the reality of a homosexual loved one.

"Within both the Christian and secular communities,
Exodus has challenged those who respond to homosexuals with ignorance and fear, and to those who uphold
homosexuality as a valid orientation. Both extremes fail
to convey the fullness of redemption found in Jesus
Christ, a gift which is available to all who commit their
life and sexuality to Him."

Exodus holds an annual conference (a "unique gath-
ering of instruction and celebration"), publishes a free
monthly newsletter, sends its leaders to speak to the
media and church groups, and "serves as the largest
Christian referral and information center regarding
homosexual issues in the world."[8]

Gay Rights Activists

The American Civil Liberties Union
(ACLU), in its own words, "has been
America's foremost advocate of indi-
vidual rights" since 1920. "The ACLU is nonpartisan. It
believes that the only way to protect freedom is to stand
fast for the idea that everyone, no matter how unpopular,
has the same rights....

"The Lesbian and Gay Rights Project is a special division of the national ACLU. It is staffed by experts in constitutional law and civil rights....

"The goal of the ACLU Lesbian and Gay Rights Project is equal treatment and equal dignity for lesbians, gay men and bisexuals. That means even-handed treatment by the government, protection from discrimination in jobs, housing, hotels, restaurants, and other public places, and fair and equal treatment for lesbian and gay couples and families....

"The Project brings 'impact' lawsuits—cases designed to have a significant effect on the lives of lesbians, gay men, and bisexuals. Project staff also write and promote laws and policies that will help achieve equality and fairness for gay people. Finally, the Project educates the public, legislators, policy makers, and opinion leaders through books, position papers, articles, lectures, and media campaigns....

"Right now, the...Project is targeting...:

"Discrimination... The Project has been fighting antigay ballot initiatives with tactical advice and campaign materials as well as with lawsuits, fighting the military's 'don't ask, don't tell' policy first in Congress then in the courts, and fighting discrimination in jobs and housing with new laws and aggressive litigation...

"Family and Relationships... The Project represents people who have been separated from their children because they are lesbian or gay, and gay men and lesbians who either want to be legally recognized as co-parents or want to adopt. Since the 1970s the ACLU has supported the right of lesbians and gay men to marry. The ACLU vigorously opposed the so-called 'Defense of Marriage' Act, and it has opposed every state law aimed at preventing lesbians and gay men from marrying. The Project has written and negotiated policies that recognize domestic partnerships, and brought cases designed to gain recognition for lesbian and gay families....

"Criminal Law Reform... The ACLU didn't give up after the U.S. Supreme Court said in *Bowers* v. *Hardwick* that states could criminalize some forms of sexual intimacy. Since that decision, the Project has been using other constitutional strategies to challenge these [sodomy] laws; the challenges will continue until all the laws have been repealed or set aside....

"Speech and Organizing... The Project has stepped in when local governments have tried to prevent lesbian and gay pride marches and other demonstrations, when schools and universities have tried to prevent lesbian and gay students from organizing, and when the state has tried to censor education about lesbians and gay men."[9]

Lambda Legal Defense and Education Fund, in its own words, "is a national organization committed to achieving full recognition of the civil rights of lesbians, gay men, and people with HIV/AIDS through impact litigation, education, and public policy work....

"Lambda carries out its legal work principally through test cases selected for the likelihood of their success in establishing positive legal precedents.... From our offices in New York, Los Angeles, Chicago, and Atlanta, Lambda's legal staff of attorneys works on a wide range of cases, with our docket averaging over fifty cases at any given time.

"Lambda also maintains a national network of volunteer cooperating attorneys, which widens the scope of our legal work and allows attorneys, legal workers, and law students to become involved in our program by working with our legal staff.

"Lambda pursues litigation in all parts of the country, in...such [areas] as discrimination in employment, housing, public accommodations, and the military; HIV/AIDS-related discrimination and public policy issues; parenting and relationship issues; equal marriage rights; equal employment and domestic partnership benefits; 'sodomy' law challenges; immigration issues; antigay initiatives; and free speech and legal protection rights.

"Lambda's work ultimately benefits all people, for it helps to fashion a society that is truly diverse and tolerant. Our overall mission to combat sexual orientation discrimination in this country has become an intrinsic part of the struggle for civil rights."[10]

Parents, Families, and Friends of Lesbians and Gays (PFLAG) describes itself as "a national nonprofit organization with a membership of over 70,000 households and more than 400 affiliates worldwide."

PFLAG "promotes the health and well-being of gay, lesbian, bisexual, and transgendered persons, their families and friends through: support, to cope with an adverse society; education, to enlighten an ill-informed public; and advocacy, to end discrimination and to secure equal rights. Parents, Families, and Friends of Lesbians and Gays provides opportunity for dialogue about sexual orientation and gender identity, and acts to create a society that is healthy and respectful of human diversity....

"Parents, Families, and Friends of Lesbians and Gays condemn the emergence of nationally orchestrated extremist groups that use religious dogma to promote bigotry and intolerance against persons with same-gender orientation—our sons and daughters and other beloved family members and friends. Some political and religious groups intend to deny our children, *forever*, the same protection guaranteed all other citizens. With spurious piety, they seek the 'special right' to force their definition of family and morality into the legal fabric of our constitution....

"We adamantly defend the rights of our gay, lesbian, and bisexual children to live in a society that accords them the same dignity, privileges, and protection accorded all other citizens."[11]

Human Rights Campaign (HRC, formerly Human Rights Campaign Fund), which calls itself "the largest national lesbian and gay political organization," envisions an America where lesbian and gay people are ensured of their basic equal rights—and can be open, honest, and safe at home, at work, and in the community. HRC has more than 250,000 members, both gay and nongay.... With a national staff, and volunteers and members throughout the country, HRC:

- lobbies the federal government on gay, lesbian, and AIDS issues;
- educates the public;
- participates in election campaigns;
- organizes volunteers;
- and provides expertise and training at the state and local level.

"Founded in 1980, HRC maintains the largest full-time lobbying team in the nation devoted to issues of fairness for lesbian and gay Americans....

"The Human Rights Campaign actively participates in every stage of the [congressional] legislative process, working to advance fair bills and to defeat efforts that would single out lesbian and gay Americans for discrimination and jeopardize their basic rights and health....

"HRC's political action committee makes financial and in-kind contributions to Republican, Democratic, and independent candidates for federal office....

"HRC has also played a key role in turning the tide against discriminatory statewide ballot measures....

President Clinton greets Human Rights Campaign
executive director Elizabeth Birch before
speaking at the organization's national dinner in
1997. President Clinton was the first president to
address such a group.

"HRC sponsors nationwide independent polling research to help demonstrate popular support for lesbian and gay equal rights and sound AIDS policies. What HRC learns from the surveys helps the organization communicate more effectively, increasing public understanding of lesbian and gay concerns in the context of America's commitment to basic fairness."[12]

Controversy in the 1990s

In the 1992 presidential election campaign, Democratic candidate Bill Clinton promised to end the ban on homosexuals in the U.S. military, appoint gays and lesbians to his administration, and support antidiscrimination legislation covering sexual orientation. By then, at least some gay rights measures enjoyed wide public support: For example, three quarters of Americans that year agreed that gays and lesbians should not be discriminated against in employment.[2]

Incumbent President George Bush, the Republican candidate, mostly sidestepped gay-related issues—but other Republicans didn't. All through the election season a runner-up for the Republican nomination, Pat Buchanan, a media commentator favored by the religious right, strongly opposed gay rights with such rhetoric as: "A visceral recoil from homosexuality is the natural reaction of a healthy society wishing to protect itself."[3] Religious right activists were prominent at the Republicans' national convention that year.

Bill Clinton won the presidency—but Democrats barely retained control of the House of Representatives, and Republicans enjoyed a slim majority in the Senate. With opposition to gay rights so strong among Republicans, gay rights initiatives seemed doomed to failure in Congress. With the notable exceptions of gays in the military (which resulted in a compromise generally seen as a failure by gay rights activists) and a few administrative appointments, the early Clinton White House didn't seriously pursue a gay rights agenda.

Locally, however, dozens of communities passed gay rights antidiscrimination measures in the early 1990s. By 1993 about one in five Americans lived in a community where some form of local or state civil rights measure protected homosexuals from discrimination.[4] At the same time, however, antigay rights initiatives were proposed in many communities. And overall, gay rights was a target increasingly favored by the religious right.

In the 1994 congressional elections, Republicans for the first time in forty years gained control of both the House and the Senate—and many state legislatures and governorships as well. Most of the victorious Republicans (including seventy-four freshmen) were backed by the Christian Coalition and other religious right organizations.

Under the leadership of Speaker of the House Newt Gingrich, Republicans asserted that the 1994 election had given them a mandate for sweeping change. Washington's concentration on the Republicans' "Contract With America" pretty much bumped gay rights from the national agenda in 1995. Meanwhile, at the state and local level, pro- and antigay rights activists clashed over dozens of antigay rights initiatives, and over the issue of gay marriage.

The 1996 presidential election featured the same partisan lineup concerning gay rights as 1992—only more so. Early on, Pat Buchanan defeated the more moderate Bob Dole in the Republican primary in New Hampshire. Although Dole eventually got the Republican nomination, the party's national convention and much of its local leadership was dominated by the religious right. The Republican party platform that year stated: "We reject the distortion of [antidiscrimination statutes] to cover sexual preference."[5]

The Democratic platform, in contrast, supported "continued efforts…to end discrimination against gay men and lesbians."[6] Nonetheless, President Clinton during the campaign signed the Defense of Marriage Act barring federal recognition of gay marriage and allowing individual states to refuse such recognition as well.

In the end, Bill Clinton was reelected president in November 1996. But Democrats gained only three House seats, and Republicans remained in control of both House and Senate.

The partisan, polarizing division between Republicans and Democrats on gay rights didn't match the American public's views on the issue. While polls have consistently shown that more than half of Americans believe that homosexual behavior is morally wrong, a much larger, growing majority of Americans has consistently endorsed at least some civil rights protections for gays and lesbians. (In a November 1996 Gallup poll, for example, the percentage of Americans favoring equal rights for homosexuals in job opportunities had grown to 84 percent.[7]) The American public had apparently reached a more nuanced and tolerant consensus on gay rights than American politicians.

The Gay Debate of 1998

In 1998, the biannual congressional elections came around once again. Early that year, Focus on the Family founder James Dobson, a prominent religious right broadcaster and publisher, warned Republicans that religious right voters would abandon the party if it didn't make "family values" issues, including homosexuality, a higher priority.[8] The religious right had worked hard for the Republican party for years and sat by while the Contract With America and other political and economic agenda items took priority. Now it was time, they said, to focus on such social issues as school prayer, abortion, and homosexuality.

That summer, apparently with an eye to shoring up support for Republicans among the religious right, the Republican-dominated House passed several antigay rights measures (none of which ultimately was signed into law) and many prominent Republicans spoke out against homosexuality. On June 15, Senate Majority Leader Trent Lott set off an avalanche of press coverage when he said on TV that homosexuality was a sin and that "in America right now there's an element that wants to make that alternative lifestyle acceptable.... You still love that person and you should not try to mistreat them or treat them as outcasts. You should try to show them a way to deal with that." Noting that his father was alcoholic, Lott added, "Others have a sex addiction or are kleptomaniacs. There are all kinds of problems and addictions and difficulties and experiences of this kind that are wrong."[9]

Later, in Lott's defense, House Majority Leader Dick Armey said, "The Bible is very clear on this.... Both myself and Senator Lott believe very strongly in the Bible." Some days later, Republican Senator Jesse Helms, a longtime outspoken enemy of homosexuality, said, "They start by pretending it's just another form of love. It's sickening." More moderate Republicans disagreed. Senator John McCain asserted, "I don't believe in discrimination of any kind," and added that gay Republicans "should be part of our party."[10]

The harsh antigay rhetoric among Republicans raised a political question: Would any gains made among voters in the fall elections by appealing to the religious right in this manner be outweighed by losses among moderate voters who might be turned off and stay home, or even vote for moderate Democrats? And to what extent would an antigay political strategy hurt Republicans by inciting more liberal, pro-gay rights Democrats to get out and vote against them?

In July 1998 a coalition of religious right organizations spent hundreds of thousands of dollars to run full-page antihomosexuality ads in newspapers across the country. One ad featured a "former lesbian" who had left behind her homosexual "lifestyle" with the help of Christian "ex-gay ministry."[11] Gay rights organizations countered with a full-page ad featuring a middle-American family with a lesbian daughter, "living proof that families with lesbian and gay kids can be whole, happy, and worthy of all that this great country promises."[12]

Critics of the "ex-gay ministries" questioned the high "cure" rates claimed by Exodus International and other ex-gay groups. They noted that psychologists and other medical authorities generally agree that sexual orientation is not a disease that can be "cured" but is instead established genetically and/or in infancy and cannot be altered, and that much of the psychological profession considers therapy aimed at changing sexual orientation to be abusive. They also pointed to the ranks of "ex-ex-gays"—individuals who attempted the ex-gay "cure" and ultimately rejected it, often after years of ex-gay "therapy." (Among those ex-ex-gays were two male founders of Exodus who fell in love and sealed their partnership with a marriage ceremony.[13])

ANTIHOMOSEXUALITY AND PRO-GAY NEWSPAPER ADS

In July 1998 a coalition of religious right organizations launched an antihomosexual ad campaign. Here are excerpts from one of their full-page newspaper ads:

Beneath a large photograph of Anne Paulk, "wife, mother, former lesbian," the ad is headlined "I'm living proof that the Truth can set you free.

"Recently, several prominent people like Trent Lott...have spoken out on homosexuality...calling it a sin. When I was living as a lesbian I didn't like hearing words like that...until I realized that God's love was truly meant for me.

"I was four years old when a teenage boy molested me. When he warned me not to say a thing, I went silent. But as I grew, the pain wouldn't stay silent....

"By the time I hit my teens I was rough...my heart cold.... I had so thoroughly rejected my own femininity that, even though I had a lot of male friends, I just wasn't attracted to men sexually....

"My sexual attraction to women blossomed in college, and after a gay counselor affirmed my feelings I joined the campus gay/lesbian group. But...I knew something was still missing. While I longed for a female life-partner, I knew it just wouldn't work. That's when I went home and prayed, 'God, please show me who You are, and fill the void in my heart.'

"Change didn't come overnight. Within six months I'd made a firm decision to forsake homosexuality, but I still had sexual desire for women. Even though I filled my days with Christian activity, I fell back into a relationship with someone who quickly became my priority in life....

"I knew I was running from God, and one day just put it to him: 'Lord, You know that I really enjoy this lifestyle, but I want You to be my first love. I need Your help. I need You to change my heart.' Shortly after that prayer, I met a Christian woman, a former lesbian, who listened patiently to my story and led me to a ministry helping people overcome homosexuality. Because they loved me without judgment, I was able to finally give all my relationships to God, and begin the real road to healing."[14]

Days after the antihomosexual ads began running, a coalition of gay rights organizations began running their response.

Beneath a photograph of a smiling father, mother, and daughter, this ad is headlined: "We're living proof that families with lesbian and gay kids can be whole, happy and worthy of all that this great country promises.

"Hello. We're Dave and Ruth Waterbury. We have two daughters whom we love very much. Margie is our lesbian daughter and she is all anyone could hope for in a child. Bright. Energetic. Successful. And a very happy young woman....

"We are a typical American family, with old roots in the heart of America. We love our church, our community and the beautiful Minnesota countryside....

"Some in this country are selling a myth that gay Americans are not people of faith. But many are deeply religious.... There are those who want to claim God and the Bible for their own narrow vision of this nation. This country was founded on religious freedom and we feel our family should have the right to embrace our daughter and our faith on an equal basis....

"The American Psychiatric Association, the American Psychological Association, and even the American Medical Association agree. Homosexuality is not a mental illness. Furthermore, they tell us gay people are just as likely to be healthy and happy as the rest of us. We were lucky. When Margie told us she was gay, we asked our family doctor for help. He said she was a normal and healthy young person. He said she was perfect just as she is. We thank God we got the right advice. All leading medical authorities agree that psychological or medical techniques aimed at conversion can be extremely damaging.

"Equality. A fair shake at life. A country free of discrimination. That is all we want for Margie. It is all anyone wants for their child. Don't buy the 'special rights' rhetoric you hear from some extremist groups these days. It's a lot of baloney. As long as our daughter can be fired no matter how good a job she is doing, something needs to change.... We happen to be Republicans. But that shouldn't matter.... Fairness should be a concern of Americans of all political stripes. It's as American as apple pie."[15]

Hate Crimes

The harsh antigay rhetoric among Republicans and the religious right raised a moral question as well: Did it encourage hate crimes against gays and lesbians?

Hate crime statistics kept by the federal government since 1990 show a steady rise in incidents targeting homosexuals. Although the quality and usefulness of these statistics are questionable, most observers believe that gay bashing has in fact increased in recent years, even as violent crime overall has decreased. Southern Poverty Law Center analysis of FBI statistics indicates that gay men and lesbians are six times as likely as Jews or Hispanics and twice as likely as blacks to be physically attacked.[16]

Just past midnight on a cold night in October 1998, a gay college student named Matthew Shepard left a bar near his school in Laramie, Wyoming, with two men he had met in the bar who had told him they were gay, too. All three got into a pickup truck driven by one of the pair, and a mile down the road the driver reportedly told Shepard: "Guess what? I'm not gay." The two strangers beat Shepard in the truck, then tied him to a fence, pistol-whipped and burned him, stole his wallet, and left him tied to the fence. A passing bicyclist found Shepard comatose and covered with blood, still tied to the fence, some eighteen hours later. Five days later, Shepard died of his injuries.[17]

Matthew Shepard's horrifying death shifted the focus of public talk about homosexuality from ex-gays and ex-ex-gays to hate crime. At the time of Shepard's death, Wyoming was one of ten states with no law specifically against hate crimes. Only twenty-one states and the District of Columbia had hate crime laws covering crimes motivated by hatred of homosexuality.[18] State hate crimes laws typically work by increasing the penalties for crimes when they are motivated by hatred. Because of this, the penalty

Matthew Shepard's murder sparked demonstrations around the country, including this shrine in New York City.

for the most awful hate crimes (like the murder of Matthew Shepard) wouldn't be increased by a hate crime law, since the penalty for murder is already maximum. Nonetheless, advocates of hate crime laws contend that they also send a message that society does not approve of bigotry and that they thus have a deterrent effect.

At the federal level, hate crime law makes federal offenses of certain crimes that would otherwise be handled locally, if the crimes are motivated by hatred. Most of the time, though, federal prosecutors allow local authorities to handle such cases; the feds intervene only rarely, when the local justice system refuses to or can't do the job properly. At the time of Shepard's death, federal hate crime law covered only race, color, religion, and national origin. President Clinton and gay rights supporters called on Congress to pass legislation expanding coverage to include sex, disability, and sexual orientation.

Shepard's death also solidified a widespread sense that antigay rhetoric had gone too far. Gay rights activists had long claimed that fire-breathing talk about "sin" and "evil" and "abomination" had encouraged hatred and violence against homosexuals. (Similar claims have been made that provocative religious right antiabortion rhetoric—"baby killer," "murderer"—encourages violence against abortion providers.) Although few would hold the religious right directly responsible for Shepard's death, the tone of such rhetoric seemed cruel and harsh in light of the young man's death. Appearance-conscious politicians put opposition to homosexuality on the back burner. And that's where it stayed, for the most part, through the November elections.

Election Results

On the Sunday before Election Day 1998, the Christian Coalition distributed millions of voter guides in churches across the United States. The guides compared candidates' positions on issues important to the religious right, including some gay rights issues. Critics contended that the guides were slanted to favor Republicans and that many issues were stated in a distorted way—referring to "affirmative action for 'sexual orientation,'" for example, rather than hate crimes or civil rights legislation.[19]

Republicans were expected to win big in 1998. Not only had the party holding the White House lost congressional seats in every mid-presidential-term election since 1934, but also Democratic President Bill Clinton was mired in the Monica Lewinsky sex scandal.

But Republicans made no gains in the Senate and actually lost a few seats in the House. Explicitly religious right Republicans lost to Democratic moderates in several key races.

Religious right activists blamed the poor Republican showing on the party's overemphasis on the Clinton sex scandal and underemphasis on the "family values" issues believed to motivate religious right voters most strongly. Other observers theorized that many moderate voters shied away from Republicans precisely because they saw both the anti-Clinton moralizing and the "family values" agenda as part of a possibly dangerous wave of religious intolerance paralyzing government and intruding into matters that should remain private. (The most aggressive seekers of presidential impeachment in the Monica Lewinsky matter were religious right Republicans who opposed gay rights and abortion and favored a moralistic "family values" agenda.)

However interpreted, the election results clearly showed the split in the Republican party between the religious right and more moderate Republican traditionalists favoring less government overall—less taxes, less regulation of business, less government intrusiveness across the board. Gay rights has been a key wedge issue at the heart of this split.

Although the 1998 election results can be read as an overall victory for moderation, they can't be read as an affirmation of gay rights. In addition to electing congress members, Hawaii and Alaska both passed measures banning gay marriages. Colorado rejected a gay rights antidiscrimination measure; so did three cities— Fayetteville, Arkansas; Fort Collins, Colorado; and Ogunquit, Maine. (A similar measure passed in South Portland, Maine.) And while both openly gay incumbent congressmen, Barney Frank (D-Mass.) and Jim Kolbe (R-Ariz.), were reelected, only one of the four openly gay newcomers seeking congressional seats won, Tammy Baldwin (D-Wisc.), .

Heading into the 2000 presidential election campaign, mainstream Republicans and Democrats alike mostly shied away from the gay rights issue. Both sides wanted to appeal to moderate voters, and neither wanted to seem captive to their party's radical fringe (pro-gay on the Democratic side, antigay on the Republican). Front-running Democrats Al Gore and Bill Bradley both generally supported gay rights but didn't make much noise about it. The Republican front-runner, George W. Bush, said he would be willing to hire a homosexual for any job for which he or she was qualified. Even Pat Buchanan, arguably the most antigay candidate in the pack, rarely mentioned homosexuality in his campaign literature and speeches, first as a Republican, then as a candidate for the Reform Party's nomination for president.

It's clear that a great many Americans disapprove of homosexual sex—but even clearer that the vast majority of Americans believe that everyone, gay as well as straight, deserves a basic level of civil rights protection. Exactly what should be included in that package of civil rights is likely to be debated well into the Twenty-first century.

Notes

INTRODUCTION
1. Randy Shilts, *Conduct Unbecoming: Gays and Lesbians in the U.S. Military* (New York: St. Martin's, 1993), p. 92.
2. James W. Button, Barbara A. Rienzo, and Kenneth D. Wald, *Private Lives, Public Conflicts: Battles Over Gay Rights in American Communities* (Washington: CQ Press, 1997), p. 63.

CHAPTER 1
1. Paul Monette, *Becoming a Man: Half a Life Story* (San Francisco: HarperSanFrancisco, 1992), p. 4.
2. Mark Thompson, ed., *Long Road to Freedom: The Advocate History of the Gay and Lesbian Movement* (New York: St. Martin's Press, 1994), p. 3.
3. David E. Newton, *Gay and Lesbian Rights: A Reference Handbook* (Santa Barbara, Calif.: ABC-CLIO, 1994), p. 35.
4. Barry D. Adam, *The Rise of a Gay and Lesbian Movement* (Boston: Twayne, 1987), p. 82.
5. James W. Button, Barbara A. Rienzo, and Kenneth D. Wald, *Private Lives, Public Conflicts: Battles Over Gay Rights in American Communities* (Washington: CQ Press, 1997), p. 26.

6. Ibid., p. 64.
7. *New York Times*, August 2, 1998, citing Gallup poll, p. 65.
8. Newton, p. 39.
9. Ibid., p. 39.
10. Ibid., p. 40.
11. Ibid., p. 40.
12. Ibid., pp. 42, 49.
13. Adam, pp. 123, 124–125.
14. Roger Magnuson, *Informed Answers to Gay Rights Questions* (Sisters, Ore.: Multnomah Books, 1994), pp. 13, 23–24, 119, 120, 122–123, 131, 143, 160–161, 164, 174.
15. Newton, p. 44.
16. Newton, pp. 51, 53, 56.
17. Button, et al., pp. 126, 127.
18. Ibid., p. 62.

CHAPTER 2

1. *New York Times*, November 25, 1998.
2. Robert M. Baird, and M. Katherine Baird, eds., *Homosexuality: Debating the Issues* (Amherst, N.Y.: Prometheus Books, 1995), p. 101.
3. *Bowers* v. *Hardwick*, excerpted in Baird, pp. 97–98.
4. Justice Blackmun's dissent in *Bowers* v. *Hardwick*, excerpted in Baird, pp. 101–102.
5. *New York Times*, November 24, 1998.
6. National Gay and Lesbian Task Force Web site (www.ngltf.org), page dated March 1999.
7. James W. Button, Barbara A. Rienzo, and Kenneth D. Wald, *Private Lives, Public Conflicts: Battles Over Gay Rights in American Communities* (Washington: CQ Press, 1997), p. 106.
8. *New York Times*, March 24, 1998, and Associated Press, March 3, 1998.
9. National Gay and Lesbian Task Force Web site (www.ngltf.org), page dated June 1999, and *New York Times*, October 4, 1999.
10. Human Rights Campaign figures cited in *New York Times*, December 2, 1998.

11. Excerpted in David E. Newton, *Gay and Lesbian Rights: A Reference Handbook* (Santa Barbara, Calif.: ABC-CLIO, 1994), pp. 113–114.
12. Excerpted in Newton, pp. 111–112.
13. Button, et al., p. 82.
14. Newton, p. 56.
15. Quoted in Newton, p. 100.
16. Newton, p. 54.
17. Ibid., p. 115.
18. Ibid., p. 45.
19. Ibid., p. 116.
20. *Romer v. Evans*, excerpted in *Facts On File*, May 23, 1996, p. 353.
21. *New York Times*, October 14, 1998.

CHAPTER 3
1. Randy Shilts, *Conduct Unbecoming: Gays and Lesbians in the U.S. Military* (New York: St. Martin's, 1993), p. 583.
2. Details cited throughout this section are found in Shilts.
3. Shilts, pp. 378–379.
4. These paragraphs on the 1980s are largely derived from Shilts, chapters 5 and 6.
5. Excerpts from Barry Goldwater's op-ed article published in *The Washington Post*, June 10, 1993, reprinted in Robert M. Baird, and M. Katherine Baird, eds., *Homosexuality: Debating the Issues* (Amherst, N.Y.: Prometheus Books, 1995), pp. 183–184.
6. Excerpted from Baird, pp. 155–156.
7. *New York Times*, April 7 and June 12, 1998.
8. Ibid., January 23, 1999.

CHAPTER 4
1. *New York Times Magazine*, December 6, 1998, p. 72.
2. All biblical quotes are from the Revised Standard Version.
3. Thomas E. Schmidt, *Straight and Narrow? Compassion and Clarity in the Homosexuality Debate* (Downers Grove, Ill.: InterVarsity Press, 1995), pp. 161–163.
4. *New York Times*, August 6, 1998.
5. Yaakov Levado, pseud., "Gayness and God: Wrestlings of

an Orthodox Rabbi," reprinted from *Tikkun* in Robert M. Baird, and M. Katherine Baird, eds., *Homosexuality: Debating the Issues* (Amherst, N.Y.: Prometheus Books, 1995), pp. 254, 261–262.

6. David E. Newton, *Gay and Lesbian Rights: A Reference Handbook* (Santa Barbara, Calif.: ABC-CLIO, 1994), p. 47.
7. Excerpted from Baird, pp. 203–208.
8. *New York Times*, November 17, 1998.
9. Barry D. Adam, *The Rise of a Gay and Lesbian Movement* (Boston: Twayne, 1987), p. 113.
10. Mel White, *Stranger at the Gate: To Be Gay and Christian in America* (New York: Simon & Schuster, 1994), pp. 148, 251, 269, 283, 284–285, 287, 293.
11. Universal Fellowship of Metropolitan Community Churches Web site, www.ufmcc.com, downloaded December 14, 1998.

CHAPTER 5
1. "The Vision and the Work of Family Research Council," a pamphlet mailed to author by FRC in November 1998.
2. William N. Eskridge, Jr., *The Case for Same-Sex Marriage: From Sexual Liberty to Civilized Commitment* (New York: Free Press, 1996), p. 46.
3. Text of final version of bill signed by president, "Defense of Marriage Act [Enrolled Bill (Sent to President)]," downloaded January 1999 from Congress's Web site at www.congress.gov.
4. Quoted in Eskridge, p. 115.
5. David E. Newton, *Gay and Lesbian Rights: A Reference Handbook* (Santa Barbara, Calif.: ABC-CLIO, 1994), p. 53.
6. Correspondence with author, January 1999.
7. National Gay and Lesbian Task Force Web site, www.ngltf.org, page dated December 1999.
8. *New York Times*, June 25, 1998.
9. Newton, p. 56.
10. *New York Times*, June 18, 1998.

11. Ibid.
12. *New York Times*, June 22 and December 22, 1998, National Gay and Lesbian Task Force press release, dated April 21, 1999.

CHAPTER 6

1. John Gallagher and Chris Bull. *Perfect Enemies: The Religious Right, the Gay Movement, and the Politics of the 1990s.* New York: Crown Publishers, 1996, p. xv.
2. Excerpted from "Families 2000 Strategy Announced by Christian Coalition," a press release dated February 18, 1998, and "Christian Coalition History, 1998," an undated press release, both sent to author by Christian Coalition in November 1998.
3. *New York Times*, August 2, 1999.
4. Focus on the Family pamphlet "Who We Are and What We Stand For," revised January 1997, sent to author by Focus on the Family in November 1998.
5. Family Research Council pamphlet "The Vision and the Work of Family Research Council," sent to author by FRC in November 1998.
6. Gary Bauer, "Beware Hidden Gay Agenda," *USA Today*, April 26, 1993, sent to author by FRC in November 1998.
7. Andrew Sullivan, *Virtually Normal: An Argument About Homosexuality* (New York: Knopf, 1995), pp. 169–170, 171, 171–172, 186–187.
8. All Exodus quotes are from a press kit sent to author by Exodus International in November 1998.
9. All quotes are from the "Lesbian and Gay Rights" section of the ACLU's Web site, www.aclu.org, downloaded in December 1998.
10. From Lambda's Web site, www.lambdalegal.org, downloaded in December 1998.
11. From PFLAG's mission statement and policy statement on "legalized discrimination," downloaded from PFLAG's Web site, www.pflag.org, in December 1998.
12. From HRC's mission statement posted on its Web site, www.hrc.org, downloaded in December 1998.

CHAPTER 7

1. Quoted in David E. Newton, *Gay and Lesbian Rights: A Reference Handbook* (Santa Barbara, Calif.: ABC-CLIO, 1994), p. 101.
2. James W. Button, Barbara A. Rienzo, and Kenneth D. Wald, *Private Lives, Public Conflicts: Battles Over Gay Rights in American Communities* (Washington: CQ Press, 1997), p. 62.
3. Quoted in Newton, p. 103.
4. Button et al., pp. 74, 76.
5. *Facts On File*, August 15, 1996.
6. Ibid., August 29, 1996.
7. *New York Times*, August 2, 1998.
8. Ibid., November 5, 1998.
9. Ibid., June 30, 1998.
10. Ibid.
11. Ibid., July 13, 1998.
12. Ibid., July 19, 1998.
13. Frank Rich, *New York Times*, July 22, 1998.
14. *New York Times*, July 13, 1998.
15. Ibid., July 19, 1998.
16. Ibid., October 13, 1998.
17. Ibid., October 10, 12, and 13, 1998.
18. Ibid., October 13, 1998.
19. "Christian Coalition Congressional Scorecard," 1998 Fall edition.

Further Information

RECOMMENDED READING

Adam, Barry D. *The Rise of a Gay and Lesbian Movement.* Boston: Twayne, 1987.

Button, James W., Barbara A. Rienzo, and Kenneth D. Wald. *Private Lives, Public Conflicts: Battles Over Gay Rights in American Communities.* Washington: CQ Press, 1997.

Gallagher, John, and Chris Bull. *Perfect Enemies: The Religious Right, the Gay Movement, and the Politics of the 1990s.* New York: Crown Publishers, 1996.

Newton, David E. *Gay and Lesbian Rights: A Reference Handbook.* Santa Barbara, Calif.: ABC-CLIO, 1994.

Shilts, Randy. *Conduct Unbecoming: Gays and Lesbians in the U.S. Military.* New York: St. Martin's, 1993.

Sullivan, Andrew. *Virtually Normal: An Argument About Homosexuality.* New York: Knopf, 1995.

White, Mel. *Stranger at the Gate: To Be Gay and Christian in America.* New York: Simon & Schuster, 1994.

ORGANIZATIONS TO CONTACT

American Civil Liberties Union (ACLU) (www.aclu.org) Lesbian and Gay Rights Project, 125 Broad Street, New York, NY 10004

Christian Coalition (www.cc.org) PO Box 1990, Chesapeake, VA 23327

Exodus International (www.exodus.base.org) PO Box 77652, Seattle, WA 98177

Family Research Council (www.frc.org) 801 G Street NW, Washington, DC 20001

Focus on the Family (www.family.org) Colorado Springs, CO 80995

Gay, Lesbian, and Straight Education Network (GLSEN) (www.glsen.org) 121 West 27th Street, Suite 804, New York, NY 10001

Human Rights Campaign (www.hrc.org) 919 18th Street NW, Washington, DC 20006

Lambda Legal Defense and Education Fund (www.lambdalegal.org) National Headquarters, 120 Wall Street, Suite 1500, New York, NY 10005

Parents, Families, and Friends of Lesbians and Gays (PFLAG) (www.pflag.org) 1101 14th Street NW, Suite 1030, Washington, DC 20005

Index

domestic partnership option, 26, 67, 81, 82

East Lansing, Michigan, 33–34
Edens, Ira A., 48
employment discrimination, 10, 12, 16, 28, 30–33, 80, 81, 85, 87
Episcopal Church, 53
evangelical Christians, 17, 18, 21
ex-gay organizations, 77, 89
Exodus International, 77, 79, 89

Falwell, Jerry, 21, 57
Families 2000 strategy, 72
Family Research Council (FRC), 61, 69, 74–77
Fayetteville, Arkansas, 96
First National Gay and Lesbian Civil Rights March on Washington, D.C. (1979), 20
Florida, 16–18, 30, 34, 69
Focus on the Family, 57, 72–74, 88
Fort Collins, Colorado, 96
Frank, Barney, *20*, 24, 96
Frost, Ruth, *58*

Gallagher, John, 70
gay pride parades, 13, *14, 15*, 81
gay rights laws, 30–34
gay rights movement
    activists, 79–84
    AIDS crisis and, 23–26

antigay political campaigns, 17–18, 20
antigay rights laws, 35–38
gay rights laws and, 30–34
marriage and family life and, 26, 61–69, 78, 96
opponents of, 17–18, 20, 21
overview of, 11–26
sodomy laws and, 27–30, 78, 81, 82
Stonewall riots (1969), *8*, 9–10, 12
Genesis 19, 49
Georgia, 29–30
Gingrich, Newt, 86
Goldwater, Barry, 44
Gore, Al, 96

Hardwick, Michael, 27, 29
Harris, Sherry, 24
hate crimes, 92, *93*, 94
Hawaii, 32, 65, 67, 96
health insurance, 62
Helms, Jesse, 88
HIV/AIDS-related discrimination, 81, 82
"Holy Union" ceremonies, 62, *63*
"Homosexual Bill of Rights," 12–13
homosexuality (*see also* gay rights movement)
    backlash against, 16–18
    church and, 52–53, *54*, 55–60, *58*
    hate crimes and, 92, *93*, 94